CRIME AND COMMUNITY IN BIBLICAL PERSPECTIVE

PLANS AND RESOURCES FOR 14 SESSIONS

KATHLEEN E. MADIGAN
AND
WILLIAM J. SULLIVAN

CRIME AND COMMUNITY IN BIBLICAL PERSPECTIVE

CRIME AND COMMUNITY IN BIBLICAL PERSPECTIVE

PLANS AND
RESOURCES FOR
14 SESSIONS

KATHLEEN E. MADIGAN
AND
WILLIAM J. SULLIVAN

Judson Press® Valley Forge

Crime and Community in Biblical Perspective

Copyright © 1980
Judson Press, Valley Forge, PA 19481

Unless otherwise indicated, Bible quotations in this volume are from the Revised Standard Version of the Bible, copyrighted 1946, 1952, 1971, 1973 © by the Division of Christian Education of the National Council of the Churches of Christ in the United States of America, and are used by permission.

Other versions of the Bible quoted in this book are:

The Holy Bible, King James Version.

The Jerusalem Bible, copyright © 1966 by Darton, Longman & Todd, Ltd. and Doubleday and Company, Inc. Used by permission of the publisher.

The New American Standard Bible, © The Lockman Foundation 1960, 1962, 1963, 1968, 1971, 1972, 1973, 1975. Used by permission.

Library of Congress Cataloging in Publication Data

Madigan, Kathleen E.
   Crime and community in Biblical perspective.

   Developed by the Judicial Process Commission as a resource for church groups.
   Bibliography: p.
   1. Justice—Biblical teaching—Study and teaching. 2. Criminal justice, Administration of—Biblical teaching—Study and teaching. I. Sullivan, William J., 1931-   joint author, II. Genesee Ecumenical Ministries. Judicial Process Commission. III. Title.
   BS680.J8M32   261.8'33   80-18469
   ISBN 0-8170-0904-3

The name JUDSON PRESS is registered as a trademark in the U.S. Patent Office.
Printed in the U.S.A. ⊕

Drawings by Sylvia Clark

This curriculum is dedicated to all those who share
the vision of Isaiah, that:

"In the wilderness justice will come to live
and integrity in the fertile land;
integrity will bring peace,
justice give lasting security.

My people will live in a peaceful home,
in safe houses,
in quiet dwellings."
—Isaiah 32:16-18 *(The Jerusalem Bible)*

Dedicated also to all those who struggle to realize the
vision, to make our land both just and safe.

BE GENTLE

Be gentle with one another—
The cry comes out of the hurting heart of humanity,
It comes from the lives of those battered with
    thoughtless words
And brutal deeds;
It comes from the lips of those who speak them,
And the lives of those who do them,
Be gentle with one another—

Who of us can look inside another and know what
    is there,
Of hope and hurt, or promise and pain?
Who can know from what far places each has come
Or to what far places each may hope to go?

Our lives are like fragile eggs—
They are brittle—
They crack and the substance escapes—
Handle with care!

Handle with exceeding, tender care for there are
    human beings within
Human beings vulnerable as we are vulnerable;
Who feel as we feel,
Who hurt as we hurt.

Life is too transient to be cruel with one another,
It is too short for thoughtlessness,
Too brief for hurting.
Life is long enough for caring,
It is lasting enough for sharing,
Precious enough for love.
Be gentle with one another.

The Reverend Richard S. Gilbert
Rochester, New York

WANTED:

CHURCH FOLK
CONCERNED ABOUT
CRIME
AND CRIMINAL JUSTICE

WHY: TO FORM A LEARNING COMMUNITY
WHEN: SUNDAY MORNINGS FOR 14 WEEKS
(OR STUDY SESSIONS OF ANY LENGTH)
WHERE: IN YOUR CHURCH
(OR, IN YOUR HOMES)

Contents

Preface

In February, 1977, Genesee Ecumenical Ministries and the Presbytery of Genesee Valley obtained funding for a criminal justice curriculum project from the United Presbyterian Synod of the Northeast and from the Monroe Foundation. Their funding proposal included the following statement of need:

> The Judicial Process Commission is the ecumenically sponsored agency in Monroe County, New York, which has been involved in study and action in response to issues in the criminal justice arena. Through the work of J.P.C. many advocacies have been developed and reform legislation written. Excellent resources have been developed to assist persons and groups to become aware of the problems associated with crime and with the responses made by the criminal justice system.

> The area of criminal justice has been one of the highest priorities in the mission of the Genesee Ecumenical Ministries and of the Presbytery since 1969, and has been the most difficult to interpret in our churches because there is little understanding among our people of the biblical and theological bases for concern in this area. We believe that a curriculum for adults in church settings would be of utmost value.

To develop the curriculum *Crime and Community in Biblical Perspective,* the Judicial Process Commission convened a group of Christian educators to serve as an editorial committee, to write the foundation papers, and to serve as a support group for the writers.

Acknowledgments: Writers: Kathleen Madigan and William Sullivan; Editor, Dixie Baker; Editorial Committee: Sara McLaughlin, chairperson, Marjorie Harding, Sarah Kohlenberg, Clare Regan, Ray Trout, Sandra Weisenreder, and Joan Wolfarth; Staff: Steven C. Law, Virginia Mackey; Editorial Assistant, Marjorie Forth; Typist, Jane Conner; Artist and Typist, Sylvia Clark.

An Overview of the Curriculum

SESSION THEMES	EDUCATIONAL METHODS	SCRIPTURE
1. "Needed: More Justice" Socioeconomic justice and prisons	1) Role-Play/simulation of inequitable situation 2) Biblical reflection on the poor in bondage	Deuteronomy 15:7-15
2. "Justice As Wholeness" The fruit of justice is peace	1) Sentence completion 2) Biblical word study 3) Suggestions for extended study: poetry-writing, art work, collage building	Isaiah 32:15-20
3. "What Is a Crime? Who Is a Criminal?" Attitudes about crime and behavioral change	1) Word association 2) Biblical reflection on Jesus' approach to "criminals"	John 8:1-11
4. "Law and Justice" Purpose of law and why people obey laws	1) Learning centers (4) 2) Guided group discussion	Matthew 18:23-35
5. "Prisons As a Social Problem" Questioning the legitimacy of prisons	1) Brainstorming 2) "Street Corner" discussion/ simulation 3) Group discussion	Matthew 7:7-12
6. "What Would a Caring Community Do?" Nature of a "caring community"	1) Web charting	Matthew 25:31-46 Revelation 3:22
7. "Justice for Victims" Exploration of victimization and the special needs of victims	1) Quiz 2) Biblical reflection: Christian response to victims	Luke 10:25-37
8. "Designing New Responses" Reconciliation in conflict situations	1) Simulation: Building sanctioning systems	2 Corinthians 5:18, 19
9. "Does the End Justify the Means?" Ethics of some law enforcement practices	1) 2 role plays 2) Group discussions	Proverbs 6:17-19

10. "Thou Shalt Not Kill" The death penalty as a moral issue	1) Opinionnaire 2) Biblical reflection on the death penalty 3) Brainstorming	Exodus 21:24 Matthew 5:38-42 Deuteronomy 30:15-20 1 Peter 2:13-14 Hosea 6:8 Romans 13:1-6
11. "Greater Love Than This" Further exploration of the moral issues surrounding the death penalty	1) Quiz 2) Role-play: Jury simulation 3) Silent meditation on Scripture	Matthew 5:43-45
12. "Alternatives to Prison"	1) Scenario and role-play: Legislative committee and public hearing	Isaiah 61:1-3 Luke 4:18-19
13. "Restoration" Mediation: The community takes charge	1) Scenario: Community panel 2) Theological and biblical reflection upon panel's decision	Leviticus 19:9-18
14. "The Need for a Vision" Preferred future	1) "Imagining" our future in light of God's design 2) Assessing strengths: Force field analysis 3) Affirmation	Isaiah 65:21-25 Revelation 21:1-4

Introduction

When serious conflicts erupt, they most frequently spring from alienation. Alienation, in turn, springs from need (the basic deprivation associated with poverty or discrimination) or from greed (the psychic and emotional deprivation associated with misplaced values). If our communities want to address and alleviate the conflicts which we now call crime, then they will have to address alienation.

How do societies respond to crime? The United States and Canada have penal-based correctional systems. That is, imprisonment is the threat or the reality behind most of the responses we make to crime. According to Irvin Waller and Janet Chin in ''Prison Use: A Canadian and International Comparison,'' published in *Criminal Law Quarterly,* December, 1974, the United States ranks highest and Canada sixth highest among fifteen industrialized nations in the number of persons per 100,000 population imprisoned. Despite the fact that we know deep down that crime springs from alienation, we generally ignore alienation as the chief cause and react punitively to the symptom, the criminal offense itself.

How can societies respond to crime and to its causal factors? This is the very dialogue which Christians must undertake. If alienation causes crime, then alienation must be addressed. If our present responses to crime are ineffective, then new responses must be generated.

This curriculum is designed to promote the dialogue. Leaders and participants are invited to:
● *form a learning community,* in which everyone is both teacher and learner.
● *look closely* at their own stereotypes, conceptions, subjective attitudes, and feelings concerning crime, victims, offenders, and the entire criminal justice system.
● *engage in a discovery process* regarding crime and justice. Each session is built to provide ample opportunity for participants and leaders to get in touch with their own knowledge and strengths and to consult with their spiritual selves in relationship to what they are experiencing.
● *develop a critical consciousness,* which for Christians

begins with our relationship to God and ends with our response to the world.
● *affirm and empower each other's ability so that* the learning community, itself, models a just community; so that the kind of world in which it is easy to be loving and just can be imagined; and so that alternative futures can be created.

This curriculum is designed to reflect biblical perspectives on justice. Each session of this curriculum is undergirded by some bold assumptions:
● Persons are created in community and for community. They have intrinsic worth and fundamental rights which belong to them as children of God, in whose image they are created (Genesis 1:27).
● The Christian concept of *justice* is related integrally to the Old Testament view of covenant and the New Testament view of Christ as Mediator of the New Covenant (Hebrews 8:6). Since God is in relationship with *all* persons, we cannot be in full community with God unless we also identify with and seek the good of all persons. Therefore, we must be biased, as God is biased, toward the hurt and oppressed (Deuteronomy 14:29; Amos 2:6). Where the needs of some are not met, the community is not whole or healthy.
● Conflict (crime) ruptures the fabric of community and is most often a symptom of alienation from that community. If that is indeed the case, then reconciliation of the offender with the victim and the community should be the goal of society's responses to such conflict.
● Therefore, retribution as the goal of legal sanctions is excluded by the Judeo-Christian ethic.
● Justice is best conceived as wholeness; that is, justice is a standard which requires society's institutions and laws to facilitate social harmony (*shalom*) and to foster the development of each person's highest possible fulfillment.

Biblical Study

Leaders and participants are encouraged to study all scriptural references. Biblical study is an important and necessary task for Christians to undertake. This curriculum approaches biblical study on two levels.

1. *Devotional.* Many persons receive comfort and joy from reading and reflection. Certainly the words of the psalmist or the teachings of Jesus (i.e., Sermon on the Mount) are inspirational in themselves. The devotional approach to the Bible can be a part of one's daily spiritual life just as theological reflection is a lifetime pursuit.

2. *Historical Investigation.* Another level of approaching biblical study is the process of examining one or more of the following categories for understanding the Scriptures in their historical setting. The bibliographic references offer the interested Bible student some basic tools for exploration.

(*a*) Historical background relates the historical/cultural situation which existed when the authors of the Bible were writing.
Bright, John, *A History of Israel.* Philadelphia: The Westminster Press, 1959.
Perrin, Norman, *The New Testament, an Introduction.* New York: Harcourt Brace Jovanovich, Inc., 1974.

(*b*) General religious and theological background reflects religious traditions from which authors of the Bible formed their theology.
Bultmann, Rudolf, *Theology of the New Testament.* vols. 1 and 2. New York: Charles Scribner's Sons, 1970.
von Rad, Gerhard, *Old Testament Theology,* vols. 1 and 2. New York: Harper & Row, Publishers, Inc., 1965.

(*c*) A study of the Bible as literature includes examination of biblical genre, i.e., prose, poetry, or parable, etc.
Jeremias, Joachim, *Rediscovering the Parables.* New York: Charles Scribner's Sons, 1966.
Tucker, Gene M., *Form Criticism of the Old Testament.* Philadelphia: Fortress Press, 1971.

(*d*) Detailed studies of a particular text include exercises in comparing various translations of the same text, word studies, and motif studies (i.e., where the idea of holiness is important, etc.).
Buttrick, George A., ed., *The Interpreter's Dictionary of the Bible,* 4 volumes. Nashville: Abingdon Press, 1962.
Young, Robert, *Analytical Concordance to the Bible.* Grand Rapids: Wm. B. Eerdmans Publishing Company, 1955.

(*e*) Commentaries aid in opening up a particular text for study.
Laymon, Charles M., ed., *The Interpreter's One-Volume Commentary on the Bible.* Nashville: Abingdon Press, 1971.

Both *devotional* and *historical investigation* of Scripture enhance one's faith and one's approach to social change. As we begin to understand the biblical message in context, possibilities for contemporary application become more apparent, and we are helped to respond as Christians to the issues confronting us in our society.

Informed by both biblical and theological assumptions, this curriculum engages participants and facilitators alike in addressing hard questions and grappling with the biblical implications of actual and possible approaches. The experiential exercises, which offer a dimension of personal involvement in issues such as victimization and sanctions, open up the possibility of new appreciation of the traumas experienced by persons directly affected by crime.

From fresh insights may come, along with broader understanding, new possibilities for solution.

Purpose of Curriculum

This curriculum is designed to empower those who participate in the learning community to:
• analyze critically present criminal laws and procedures of the criminal justice system;
• evaluate criminal justice in light of Judeo-Christian perspectives on justice righteousness (*tsedeqah*) and caring community (*shalom*); specifically, biblical concepts of creative justice described by theologian Paul Tillich as "listening, loving, and forgiving";
• work for more effective approaches to the reconciliation of offender, victim, and community—approaches including alternatives to arrest, prosecution, and imprisonment; and
• acknowledge and respond to their own responsibilities and abilities to contribute to the building of a safe and viable community.

Use of Curriculum

This 14-week curriculum is written as a coherent whole: one session builds on another. The learning community is encouraged, therefore, to use all sessions. If this is not possible, in either Sunday morning class settings or in study groups meeting at times other than Sunday mornings, keep in mind that Session 2 is essential because it contains the central theme of "justice as wholeness." If only six sessions can be covered, we suggest sessions 2, 3, 4, 6, 7, and 14.

Each session in this book has three basic kinds of resources. The session outline provides direction for the leader for the activities to be used. Handout material can be duplicated and given to participants. Background reading supplies information about the basic theme.

So long as the facilitator for the learning community is faithful to the purpose of the curriculum, to the objectives for each session, and to the theological assumptions, flexibility in adapting the curriculum to the group is encouraged.

Education for social change requires that a sense of community be developed among all who are engaged in the learning process. Use the suggestions for enrichment. Plan a potluck supper, a session for presenting art work, time for liturgies.

Leave some time for feedback at the end of each session. Help each member of the group feel comfortable about expressing feelings about either the content or the group process.

JUSTICE

JUSTICE

JUSTICE

justice

justice

JUSTICE

Justice

JUSTICE

JUS

SESSION 1—Needed: More Justice

SCRIPTURE: Deuteronomy 15:7-15

TIME: 45 minutes to 1 hour

PURPOSE: To increase participant's understanding of the economic and social injustices in society and how these injustices are related to criminal justice.

OBJECTIVES

1. To explore social and economic injustice experientially and in reflection.
2. To have participants consider why it is more often the poor and oppressed who get caught up in the criminal justice system.
3. To reflect on the above from a biblical perspective.

LEADER PREPARATION

Materials needed:

Newsprint, markers, masking tape   Name tags
Pencils   Identity cards
Broken pencils
Course outline (See Overview of the Curriculum)
Bible or copies of Deuteronomy 15:7-15

Advance Preparation

1. Prepare Newsprint Chart 1, "Session at a Glance." Having this agenda in view will help the whole group stay within the time frame.

```
             SESSION AT A GLANCE
Introductory Exercise                 5 minutes
Reflection          (small group)     5 minutes
                    (group sharing)   5 minutes
Small Group Discussion               20 minutes
   "Economic and Social Justice"
Reporting and Session Summary      5-20 minutes
Looking Toward the Next Session       5 minutes
```

2. Prepare Newsprint Chart 2 by writing "FEELINGS" at the top of a sheet of newsprint. Prepare Chart 3 by writing "WHAT'S WRONG" at the top of another sheet. Prepare Chart 4 following the example given in the Session Outline.

3. Prepare "identity cards" for each participant. Make the "identities" reflect the following characteristics found in society: (1/3 of your group will be poor; 2/3 will be non-poor)

30 percent Poor—with income below the 1979 subsistence level of $9,600 per year for a family of four (some 60 million persons in the United States)

70 percent Non-Poor—some 140 million persons

(Sample of identity card)

> I am a member of a minority group and poor. My income is _____.

4. Duplicate copies of Handouts 1 and 2.

5. Arrange the room so that there are sufficient tables labeled "Non-Poor" and chairs at the front of the room for those with "identities" above the poverty level. At each place have a sharpened pencil. At the back of the room have one table labeled "Poor" (in worn condition, if possible) and insufficient chairs for those with "identities" at the poverty level. Have only one or two broken pencils at that table.

SESSION OUTLINE

As the Session Begins (5 minutes)

As participants enter the room, give each a name tag and an "identity card." Tell them to read about themselves on their identity cards. Ask them to go to the appropriate table, where they are to write their names on their name tags—the "Non-Poor" to the front; the "Poor" to the back of the room.

Allow participants to experience this arrangement for about 5 minutes. Make no comments yourself, but listen for the remarks of the participants to bring them out during the total group discussion time. If anyone at the back table goes to another room to bring in additional chairs, "arrest" him or her for stealing. Do nothing if someone from a front table should try to help someone from the back. Any poor or minority person who does anything to correct the situation should cause you to react negatively (i.e., harass the person, ask what he or she is doing, etc.), but you should not react negatively to similar attempts from the non-poor "middle-class" persons in front.

The point of this exercise is to allow the participants to experience a situation that is fundamentally unjust and to contrast that with a biblical conception of justice that requires that the needs of *all* persons be met. Just as society does not provide adequately for the needs of poor persons or for those of many minority group members, so you have not provided for the needs of those so designated in the group.

Reflection

After the exercise is completed, ask the participants to share their feelings about this exercise in groups of two or three. Allow 5 minutes for sharing in small group, then 5 minutes for sharing with the total group.

Post Newsprint Charts 2 and 3. Use them to list the responses of the participants. The "feelings" list may include anger, frustration, confusion, especially from those designated as poor or members of minority groups. Expressions of "what's wrong" may include that the arrangement of chairs and equipment is unfair and inequitable. The situation was structured so that those who are "poor" could not participate fully in the learning experience.

Next, if someone from the front table hasn't already suggested that those from the back table join them, ask for a "remedy" to the situation, hoping to elicit such a suggestion.

Small Group Discussion (20 minutes)
"Economic and Social Justice"

Have the participants break into small groups of three to five persons. Post Newsprint Chart 4.

INSTRUCTIONS FOR SMALL GROUP
DISCUSSION
- Appoint a spokesperson.
- Read aloud Deuteronomy 15:7-15.
- Distribute Handouts 1 and 2 and reflect briefly as individuals on them.
- Engage in discussion.

Ask if these instructions are clear. Allow 20 minutes for this section. Give a 2-minute warning before discussion should end.

Reporting and Session Summary (5 to 20 minutes)

Ask each spokesperson to report one insight from the small group's discussion to the total group. Record the insights on newsprint (you may want to use this listing in later sessions). Record insights from each group before engaging in response or total group discussion.

Leave time for a summary statement by you about the participants' reaction to the opening exercise and to the reflection and discussion sheet.

Looking Toward the Next Session (5 minutes)

Give participants a course outline, if they do not yet have it, and make announcements pertaining to Session 2, "Justice As Wholeness."

"ECONOMIC AND SOCIAL JUSTICE"
For Reflection and Discussion

Instructions: Reflect briefly, individually, on this material. You will have 15 minutes to engage in discussion with others in your group. At the end of that time, your spokesperson will report one insight from your discussion to the total group.

"If there is among you a poor man, one of your brethren, in any of your towns within your land which the LORD your God gives you, you shall not harden your heart or shut your hand against your poor brother, but you shall open your hand to him, and lend him sufficient for his need, whatever it may be" (Deuteronomy 15:7-8).

For the past three decades, the proportion of income received annually by each fifth of the population has remained virtually the same:

Income Fifths	1947	1973[1]
Wealthiest Fifth	43%	41%
Next Fifth	23%	24%
Middle Fifth	16%	17%
Fourth Fifth	11%	12%
Poorest Fifth	5%	5%

Even more telling is the distribution of wealth, which includes economic assets (homes, cars, stocks, bonds, etc.):

Wealth Fifths	Percent Owned[2]
Wealthiest Fifth	76%
Next Fifth	15.5%
Middle Fifth	6.2%
Fourth Fifth	2.1%
Poorest Fifth	.2%

Consider: The Deuteronomist admonishes the Israelites to provide for those among them who are in need. The same message is clearly echoed throughout the Scriptures. How might we apply this message to our own lives and society?

*   *   *   *   *

"If your brother, a Hebrew man, or a Hebrew woman, is sold to you, he shall serve you six years, and in the seventh year you shall let him go free from you. And when you let him go free from you, you shall not let him go empty handed . . ." (Deuteronomy 15:12-13).

In the United States:
25 million to 50 million persons are classified as poor (20-40%).
15% are members of minority groups.
15% have not graduated from high school.[3]
In the prisons of the United States:
75% are poor.
44% are members of minority groups.
80% have not graduated from high school.[4]

Consider: These points imply that those among us who are in need (especially the poor and members of minority groups) are disproportionately caught up in the criminal justice system. What does the message of the Deuteronomist say to us?

*   *   *   *   *

"You shall remember that you were a slave in the land of Egypt, and the LORD your God redeemed you; therefore, I command you this today" (Deuteronomy 15:15).

According to Eugene Doleschal, director of the National Council on Crime and Delinquency Information Center, Hackensack, New Jersey, in a letter dated July 19, 1978, the findings of more recent studies are essentially the same. He says:

Hidden crime studies (self-report studies) have generally found that all of us have committed some kind of an offense which could have resulted in a sentence of incarceration. More importantly, they have found that serious and habitual offending is not confined to a specific group of the population (such as the poor) but that is equally distributed among all socioeconomic groups.

In one study of middle-class persons, 90% of the respondents admitted having broken the law:
37% admitted evading taxes
11% had committed robbery
26% had stolen a car
89% admitted to larceny
The average number of crimes per person was 18![5]

Consider: Does our society have a double standard for holding people responsible for acts which they have committed? If so, what does that say about justice?

---

[1]J. H. Turner and C. D. Sturnes, *Inequality: Privilege and Poverty in America* (Pacific Palisades, Calif: Goodyear Publishing Co., 1976), p. 51.

[2]Board of Governors of the Federal Reserve System, *Survey of Financial Characteristics of Consumers* (Washington, D.C.: Government Printing Office, 1962), cited in J. H. Turner, *Social Problems in America* (New York: Harper & Row, Publishers, Inc., 1977), p. 190.

[3]U.S. Bureau of the Census, 1970. Figures on education: Current Population Series P-20, #314, "Educational Attainment in the United States, 1976-77," issued in December, 1978.

[4]*The Witness*, publication of the Episcopal Church, 1977.

[5]James Wallerstein and Clement Wyle, "Our Law-Abiding Lawbreakers," *Probation*, April, 1947.

Most studies of the causes of crime in this decade, whether contained in sociological texts, high-level governmental commission reports, or best-selling books . . . lament the disproportionately high arrest rate for blacks and poor people and assert with wearing monotony that criminality is a product of slums and poverty. [One such book] invites the reader to mark on his city map the areas where health and education are poorest, where unemployment and poverty are highest, where blacks are concentrated—and he will find these areas also have the highest crime rate.

Hence the myth that the poor, the young, the black, the Chicano are indeed the criminal type of today is perpetuated, whereas in fact crimes are committed, although not necessarily punished, at all levels of society.

There is evidence that a high proportion of people in all walks of life have at some time or other committed what are conventionally called "serious crimes." A study of 1,700 New Yorkers weighted toward the upper income brackets, who had never been arrested for anything, and who were guaranteed anonymity, revealed that 91 percent had committed at least one felony or serious misdemeanor. The mean number of offenses per person was 18. Sixty-four percent of the men and 27 percent of the women had committed at least one felony, for which they could have been sent to the state penitentiary. Thirteen percent of the men admitted to grand larceny, 26 percent to stealing cars, and 17 percent to burglary. . . . Thus it seems safe to assert that there is indeed a criminal type—but he is not a biological, anatomical, phrenological, or anthropological type; rather, he is a social creation, etched by the dominant class and ethnic prejudices of a given society.

From *Kind and Usual Punishment: The Prison Business,* by Jessica Mitford (New York: Alfred A. Knopf, Inc., 1973), pp. 51-52, 56.

SESSION 1—BACKGROUND READING

Needed: More Justice

Job pondered the hard questions of justice and injustice while sitting on a dung heap. Most of us have not experienced severe injustice, let alone the extremes suffered by Job. Consequently, we seldom have to reflect on what is or is not fundamentally just. For this reason we probably assume that our institutions charged with administering justice in our names are doing an able job. We know that the welfare system tries to rescue the neediest from extreme want while the criminal justice system labors to address the problems of crime.

However, *closer scrutiny of our institutions reveals that injustice is built into our social system and can be seen in the unequal way that we distribute the resources needed for a fully human existence.* Because of unequal distribution mighty power resides with those who possess wealth; powerlessness is the hallmark of the poor. By our acceptance of the traditional approaches of institutions, we concur that it is inevitable for generation after generation to subsist on welfare, for our infant mortality rate to remain scandalously high, and for millions to struggle on with inadequate education and health care. Across the board there has been a shortchanging of the poor in the basic life chances that the majority take for granted.

In our adversary system of criminal justice, when attorneys fight cases before a judge and perhaps a jury, there is little hope that the poor person will be represented as well as the wealthy one. Generally, poor people have to accept whatever free legal help is available to them. Wealthier persons may have a whole battery of expensive lawyers arguing their cases. The most casual look at the final disposition of cases involving both the haves and the have-nots who are caught up in our criminal justice system shows the reality of this assessment. Where better to look than in our jails and prisons? On the face of things, most criminal acts would appear to be committed by young, poor persons, a large percentage of whom are members of minority groups.

We respond much more frequently and harshly to crimes which poor and powerless persons commit. White collar crime—committed with the pencil or the computer or through other job theft—accounts for far more dollar loss per year than do the more visible street crimes—the muggings, car thefts, and robberies that plague us. Yet few white collar "criminals" are imprisoned. The rich and clever who plunder a state's treasury or a corporation's assets almost never serve time in prison.

This consideration of whom we convict or exonerate, put in prison or on probation, indicates how unequal our distribution of "justice" is. Why then is there so little outcry against this double standard? Could it be that most of us look to the law to protect what we have—our property, our possessions, and our freedom to enjoy them? We do not perceive that our private property is threatened by the public official who takes bribes or raids the till or by the corporate thief in spite of the fact that such larceny adds to the cost of almost everything we buy as well as to our taxes.

What frightens and angers us most are the muggers leaping out at us in the dark; the dope-driven addict whose cravings have blurred all human consideration; or juvenile thieves, often too hardened by a childhood lacking stability, to care whom they hurt. Could it be that we indicate to our elected officials and to criminal justice personnel that these are the persons we want caught and punished because we fear that what we have is threatened—all the elements of a life of hard work and what the inherited advantages of good health, education, and security have made possible?

Usually we would rather not look beyond this understandable response to illegal and antisocial behavior to the harder questions of causation, particularly those of economic and social justice. Our society's attempts at reaching out to the poor fall short. The military and other priorities of our government keep our public expenditures well short of the massive commitment to social change that could truly make a difference. Warheads and fighter planes are bought at the price of health care and a national commitment to jobs. *The first session plan of this curriculum is designed to help participants under-*

stand the relationship between these failures and the problem we call crime.

Citizenship in a nation like ours, built on the concept of justice for all, should alone be enough to motivate us to seek a better way of dealing with the problems we discuss. Add to that reason the more rigorous demands that accompany faith in Jesus Christ, and the call for justice becomes even stronger. Jesus envisioned a far better society than ours when he cited, in the synagogue at Nazareth, the prophet Isaiah:

> *"The Spirit of the Lord is upon me,*
> *because he has anointed me to preach good news*
> *to the poor,*
> *He has sent me to proclaim release to the captives*
> *and recovering of sight to the blind,*
> *to set at liberty those who are oppressed,*
> *to proclaim the acceptable year of the Lord."*
>
> —*Luke 4:18*

Our task is to fulfill that vision. How can we preach that gospel to the poor and leave them the least desirable housing, the worst schools, the most overburdened attorneys, and then condemn many of them to prisons? Throughout the Bible, we are continually reminded that the community of faith has a special debt of justice owed to the oppressed.

History offers few examples of worse injustice than what the Israelites confronted in Egypt. Because God came to their rescue at their most serious moment of need, they were expected to care for the needy in their midst.

"Concern for others" in the Judeo-Christian tradition (covenant, prophets, and the teachings of Jesus) finds expression in concern for the most oppressed.

Insofar as we tolerate the exploitation of the most vulnerable, we part from the demands of the covenant in Deuteronomy, the prophets, and the New Testament. Does this mean we are called to bring perfect justice to our society? No. Rather, we are called to do our best and never to lose our measure of biblical intolerance for the evil that is injustice. As Christians mindful of our roots, we will want to champion the rights of all persons. To do this, it is necessary to look critically at how society protects us and our possessions. Is the security that most enjoy purchased at the cost of equal opportunity and equality before the law for those who have little or nothing?

Wherever injustice occurs, we cannot lose sight of the necessity of bringing temporary relief to the immediate needs of our brothers and sisters or of the need to work earnestly toward changing and making more responsive the institutions within our society that are our vehicles for dealing justly with each other.

* * * * *

Notes on Scripture: Historical Investigation

1. *Cultural Conditions*

To begin setting the historical stage for Deuteronomy, we must look at the reign of Manasseh, king of Judah (687–642 B.C.). Manasseh reigned in Judah just before Josiah, and it was during Josiah's reign that the Book of Torah or Deuteronomy was found in the temple.

Manasseh's reign is referred to as Judah's Dark Age. During Manasseh's reign Assyria was the dominating world power, and he capitulated to Assyria so as not to rock the boat and lose his power. Second Kings 21 points out Manasseh's acts: he rebuilt high places, erected altars to Baal, made an emblem of Asherah (child sacrifice), to name a few. His acts placed an official stamp of approval on Assyrian religious practices, and the people of Judah were thrown into a state of confusion.[1]

Josiah became king in the midst of this confusion. By this time, however, Assyria was beginning to lose its power and Josiah inherited the job of unifying Israel, did ". . . right in the eyes of the Lord, and walked in all the way of David his father . . ." (2 Kings 22:2).

2. *Discovery of the Book of Torah (Deuteronomy)*

Second Kings 22:3-8 is a historian's account of the discovery of "the book of the law" during the eighteenth year of Josiah's reign. Most scholars agree that this is the book of Deuteronomy.[2] As Bernhard Anderson points out, it was no accident that repairs were being made to the temple when the book was found. Josiah had already begun efforts to abolish Assyrian influence, and the discovery of a book reflecting the faith of the Fathers was significant with regard to Josiah's unifying efforts.

3. *The Use of Earlier Traditions*

Deuteronomy reflects the faith of early Israel in many ways. However, the traditions have been transformed to speak to Israel during Josiah's reign. In Deuteronomy 15:1-4 and 12-18, we find two such traditions. Deuteronomy 15:1-4 says: *"At the end of every seven years you shall grant a release. And this is the manner of the*

[1]Bernhard W. Anderson, *Understanding the Old Testament*, 2nd ed. (Englewood Cliffs, N.J.: Prentice-Hall, Inc., 1966), pp. 337-338. Reprinted by permission.

[2]John Bright, *A History of Israel* (Philadelphia: The Westminster Press, 1959), p 297. See pages 294-302 for Bright's exposition of Israel's history during the reign of Josiah.

release: every creditor shall release what he has lent to his neighbor. . . . But there will be no poor among you (for the Lord will bless you in the land which the Lord your God gives you for an inheritance to possess)." In Exodus 23:10, we read an account of the earlier tradition: "For six years you shall sow your land and gather in its yield; but the seventh year you shall let it rest and lie fallow, that the poor of your people may eat. . . ." In Exodus the sacral tradition is directed toward agrarian people in an earlier stage of Israel's development. It comes to us in Deuteronomy after the rise of the monarchy and the development of currency and taxes. Instead of land lying fallow, one is required to release one's neighbors from debt. Deuteronomy 15:12-18 is a similar transformation of a tradition concerning release of slaves (see Exodus 21:1-11 in comparison).

4. Contemporary Application

During the reign of Manasseh, Israel became confused by the influx of foreign religion which did not have the ethical concerns for the poor demanded by the faith of Israel. Besides worshiping idols (Baal, etc.), there existed an obvious neglect of the poor and weak.

Josiah and a faithful remnant remembered a time when Israel's greatness was defined by relationship to Yahweh. This covenant relationship required *more justice*. The author of Deuteronomy was compelled to look to the traditions of Israel's past to provide a unity of perspective for considering human action. The transformation of these traditions served to bring structures and institutions in society under the judgment of *ultimate norms*.

When we consider our present criminal justice system, we hear a call: needed, more justice! As we shall discover, our Christian heritage provides us with a response. We, like Josiah, have the challenge of restoring justice to our land by affirming the ultimate norms of the faith which we profess.

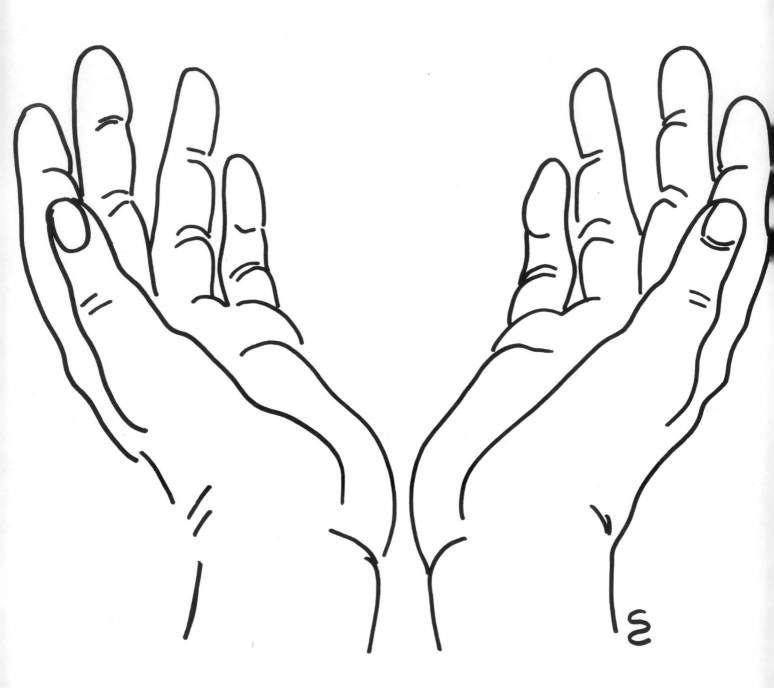

SESSION 2—Justice As Wholeness

SCRIPTURE: Isaiah 32:15-20

TIME: 45 minutes to 1 hour

OBJECTIVE

To explore concepts of justice that would undergird reconciling communities.

LEADER PREPARATION

Materials needed:

Newsprint, markers, masking tape
Copies of Isaiah 32:16-18
Paper and pencils
Craft materials (if there is time for enrichment through artistic expression)

If possible, copies of Bible concordances; John McKenzie's *Dictionary of the Bible;* Alan Richardson's *A Theological Word Book of the Bible;* Hugh White's *Shalom in the Old Testament.*

Advance Preparation

1. Prepare Newsprint Chart 1.

SESSION AT A GLANCE

Justice: Word Association	1 minute
Total Group Sharing	4 minutes
Justice and Peace: Word Studies	20 minutes
Total Group Sharing and Session Summary	15 to 30 minutes
Looking Toward the Next Session	5 minutes

---

2. Copy on newsprint or have duplicated the following Bible passage:

> *In the wilderness justice will come to live*
>   *and integrity in the fertile land;*
> *integrity will bring peace,*
>   *justice give lasting security.*
>
> *My people will live in a peaceful home,*
>   *in safe houses,*
> *in quiet dwellings.*
>
> —Isaiah 32:16-18 *(The Jerusalem Bible)*

3. Prepare Newsprint Charts 2, "Justice is . . . ," 3, "Instructions for Word Study," and 4, "Summary Questions." See the Session Outline for descriptions of each.

4. Duplicate Handouts 1 and 2 for each member.

5. If you have access to the book, read pages 651, 652, and 739-741 from McKenzie's *Dictionary of the Bible* and Hugh White's *Shalom in the Old Testament* (United Church Press).

SESSION OUTLINE

Justice: Word Association (1 minute)

Allow one minute for each person to write on a piece of paper all the words that come to his or her mind when the word "justice" is mentioned.

Total Group Sharing (4 minutes)

Post Newsprint Chart 2, "JUSTICE IS. . . ." (a sheet of newsprint with "Justice Is. . . ." written at the top). Ask members of the group to share their associations/feelings about justice and record them on the newsprint. Encourage no interaction on the words at this time, but keep this newsprint posted. Allow four minutes for this sharing.

Justice and Peace: Word Studies (20 minutes)

Post Newsprint Chart 3:

Instructions for Word Study
1) Reflect individually on the Bible passage.
2) Read definitions of *tsedeqah* and *shalom,* and the paper by Paul L. Hammer (Handouts 1 and 2).
3) Write group definition of key words *tsedeqah* and *shalom.*
4) Record your definitions and insights on newsprint for posting.

Explain to the participants that a word study focuses on key words in a biblical passage in order to shed light on the passage. In this instance, we will be studying how the writers of Isaiah typically thought of *justice* and *peace*.

Note: When working with the key words, *tsedeqah* and *shalom*, it is important to keep in mind that various translations differ. In *The Jerusalem Bible, tsedeqah* is translated as "integrity"; in RSV as "righteousness," in the *New American Bible* as "goodness." *Shalom*, by the same token, is sometimes translated by words other than "peace." This points up the need to understand the writer's meaning and the "essence" of each Hebrew word.

Tell the group members that they will engage in word study for 20 minutes and have 10 minutes for sharing their insights in the total group.

Ask the participants to break into groups of three to five persons. Distribute biblical materials, newsprint, and markers.

Refer to Newsprint Chart 3 for directions. After 15 minutes give a 5-minute warning.

Total Group Sharing and Session Summary (15 minutes)

Ask one member of each group to post the group's definitions and insights and to make clarifying comments.

Post Newsprint Chart 4 as below and engage participants in discussion of the Summary Questions.

SUMMARY QUESTIONS
1) Which words and phrases from the Word Association Study (Justice is . . .) done earlier would fit into your group definitions of *tsedeqah* and *shalom* (justice and peace)?
2) Which would not fit? Why not?
3) If some words or phrases do not fit into your group definitions, what concepts are they defining?
4) Under which concept of justice would you prefer to live?

If summary is needed, point out that *tsedeqah* (Isaiah 32:16-18) is a biblical concept of justice which has to do with wholeness in our relationships with God and with each other. It encompasses a concern for equity and need. A whole community is one in which the needs of all persons are met and in which each person is empow-

ered to find his or her highest possible fulfillment. The prophets were well aware of this covenantal requirement and warned their communities of the consequences if they continued in their failure to meet the needs of the oppressed among them. God's justice is biased toward the poor and oppressed because, where the needs of some persons are not met, the community is not whole or healthy.

The outcome of justice is peace (Isaiah 32:17). Harmony, wholeness, peace (*shalom*) is a product of just social relationships.

Looking Toward the Next Session (5 minutes)

1. For enrichment, or if time allows in this session, post the following list of additional passages containing key words:

Shalom Leviticus 26:3-8; Psalm 85:8-13; Isaiah 9:2-7; 60:17-18; Ezekiel 34:25-26; 37:26-28.

Tsedeqah Genesis 15:1-6; Deuteronomy 24:10-15; Amos 5:21-24; Isaiah 11:1-5; 42:6-9; 61:10-11; Jeremiah 22:3. Suggest checking a biblical concordance for further passages.

2. Suggest rereading Isaiah 32:15-20 during the week and the writing of a modern paraphrase which can be posted in Session 3.

3. Encourage each person to create some kind of artistic image of the concept of justice. This could be a painting, a sculpture, a poem, a tapestry, a slide presentation, a mobile, a photo-essay, etc. You may have materials on hand, such as clay, pipe-cleaners, paints, write-on slides, etc.

Ask that their creations be put on display either in your meeting room or, if possible, in a "gallery" somewhere in the church.

For those interested in poetry but afraid to begin, here are two simple forms of poetry which most people can enjoy writing:

Cinquain: a poetry form developed in France. Each poem has five lines:
Line 1: Theme or title (one word)
Line 2: Two words about the title
Line 3: Three words or a phrase about the title
Line 4: Four-word descriptive phrase
Line 5: A synonym for the title
Example:

Christmas
Snowy, peaceful
Wondrous, anticipation-filled
Baking, present-giving, rejoicing
Noel!

Example:

Easter
Resurrection Day
Jesus is alive
Glorious gift of God
Victory!

Haiku: a type of Japanese poetry. There are three lines, with a total of seventeen syllables. All three lines express a single thought:

Line 1: 5 syllables   Together, waves, sand
Line 2: 7 syllables   And I, discover shells, made
Line 3: 5 syllables   Captives of the shore.

4. Suggest that each person begin to look for justice-related newspaper articles, headlines, short magazine articles, or pictures to bring to class. These could be used to create a collage which will grow with each session.

From: *A Theological Word Book of the Bible,* edited by Alan Richardson (New York: Macmillan, Inc., 1971). Copyright 1950 by Macmillan Publishing Co., Inc., renewed 1978 by Macmillan Publishing Co., Inc. Reprinted with permission of Macmillan Publishing Co., Inc.

JUSTICE

"It is noteworthy that this word is not found in NT, and rarely in OT. Where it is found . . . it represents the word translated 'judgment' *(q.v.)* once, and elsewhere (27 times) one of the two forms of the word usually translated 'righteousness' *(q.v).*" (p. 119, N.H. Snaith)

RIGHTEOUS, RIGHTEOUSNESS

"The twin Heb. words *tsedeq* and *tsedaqah* are regularly translated by 'righteousness' . . . though occasionally the rendering is 'justice.' Originally they signified that which conforms to the norm, and for the Hebrews this norm is the character of God himself. The idea conveyed by the words is certainly ethical, but there is a steady tendency towards the idea of salvation. This is due, in the first instance, to the writings of the 8th-cent. prophets.

"It is true that these 8th-cent. prophets, Amos, Hosea, Isaiah and Micah, were ethical prophets, for they insisted with the utmost firmness and resolution upon right action and fair dealing between man and man. They all make charges of glaring injustice, bribery and corruption, in the courts, and Micah even goes so far as to charge the rich with 'skinning' the common people (3.2f.). . . . this emphasis works out from the 8th cent. onwards in making it more and more clear that if God is going to see righteousness established in the land, he himself must be particularly active as 'the helper of the fatherless' (Ps. 10:14) to 'deliver the needy when he crieth; and the poor that hath no helper' (Ps. 72:12).

"Righteousness involves the establishment of equal rights for all, and to this extent 'justice' is a sound equivalent. The word is actually used in the sense of giving judgment, and God does judge righteously (Ps. 7:8-11), though at the same time it is remarkable how, even in passages where God is spoken of as judge, there is the reference to the poor and the needy on one side and 'the person of the mighty' on the other (cf. Lev. 19:15). All this means that if justice be taken to mean no more than strict equality, then the word in the main is inadequate.

". . . in the Pauline Epistles the word righteousness is used in three main senses: first, of that ethical conduct which is demanded by the Mosaic Law; second, of the salvation which is the gift of God through Christ; third, of that ethical conduct which is demanded of the Christian, that which involves as its minimum ethical demands all that is included in turning the other cheek and going the second mile, or that which is contained in the statement that we are unprofitable servants even though we have done that which it was our duty to do (Luke 17:10)." (pp. 202-204, N.H. Snaith)

PEACE

"The word *eirēnē* (peace) in classical Gk. is primarily negative, denoting absence or end of war. . . . But generally the biblical sense of 'peace' is determined by the positive conception of the Heb. word *shalom* . . .

"*Shalom* is a comprehensive word, covering the manifold relationships of daily life, and expressing the ideal state of life in Israel. Fundamental meaning is 'totality' (the adjective *shalem* is translated 'whole'), 'well being,' 'harmony,' with stress on material prosperity untouched by violence or misfortune. Peace is 'the untrammelled, free growth of the soul [i.e., person] . . . harmonious community; the soul can only expand in conjunction with other souls . . . harmony, agreement, psychic community . . . every form of happiness and free expansion, but the kernel of it is the community with others, the foundation of life.'" (p. 165, C. F. Evans)

SESSION 2   Handout 2

NEW TESTAMENT PERSPECTIVES ON JUSTICE AND PEACE

Paul L. Hammer, Professor of New Testament
Colgate Rochester/Bexley Hall/Crozer
Divinity Schools

New Testament perspectives on justice and peace of course have their primary roots in the Hebrew Bible (Old Testament) and in the heritage of Israel. The Exodus event and theme—liberation out of bondage—called Israel to be a liberated and liberating people, the servants of God's justice and peace, righteousness, and truth.

For New Testament writers generally (we need to be careful not to oversimplify their richness and diversity), that liberation theme continues and climaxes in Jesus. "For freedom Christ has set us free" (Paul). "So if the Son makes you free, you will be free indeed" (John). "The spirit of the Lord is upon me, because he has anointed me to preach good news to the poor. He has sent me to proclaim release to the captives and recovering of sight to the blind, to set at liberty those who are oppressed" (Luke's portrayal of Jesus reading from the prophet Isaiah).

Again generally, for New Testament writers liberation calls for justice and without justice there can be no peace—no *shalom:* wholeness, harmony, health; and without righteousness (i.e., making relationships right), there can be no truth. In fact, New Testament writers see in Jesus, a human life lived in history, the truth of God that reaches out seeking to make all relationships right and just and thereby to bring peace.

But is not all such language simply "spiritual" and intended to speak only of the personal and private relationship of individuals with God? Yes, it does include that element. Yet to limit it to the personal and private would be to distort utterly the New Testament witnesses. They include also social and public relationships; and unless the relationship with God expresses itself in interpersonal and social concern, it is regarded as phony and hypocritical. "If any one says, 'I love God,' and hates his brother, he is a liar" (1 John 4:20). And any super religiosity bent only on rule keeping, that neglects "the weightier matters of the law, justice and mercy and faith" (Matthew 23:23), receives Jesus' scathing denunciation.

The uncompromising integrity of Jesus' own love and caring for outcast persons and social groups (shepherds and criminals, tax collectors and soldiers, prostitutes and Samaritans, lepers and beggars, etc.), his standing for God's reign of justice and peace, led to conflict with both religious and political authorities and finally to his crucifixion. Yet out of such a life and death comes God's power of resurrection, of new creation and new life, intended for all the world's peoples. That is a basic New Testament affirmation.

In New Testament perspective, criminal justice is not a simple balancing-of-the-scales, retributive kind of justice. It is a right-making, reconciling justice that promises "release to the captives" and "liberty to the oppressed," that reaches out even on the cross to a criminal (in Luke), that seeks wholeness, *shalom,* for every individual person and for the social and institutional structures of all human relationships. It calls for a loving and caring, healing and reconciling community, wherein all God's children may know their full humanity.

BIBLIOGRAPHY FOR BIBLE STUDY

Bible Atlases

May, Herbert G., and Hunt, G. H., eds., *Oxford's Bible Atlas.* New York: Oxford University Press, 1974.

Terrien, Samuel, *The Golden Book Bible Atlas.* New York: Golden Press, 1973 (good for children).

Wright, George E., and Filson, Floyd V., eds., *Westminster Historical Atlas to the Bible.* Philadelphia: The Westminster Press, 1956.

Bible Dictionaries

Buttrick, George A., ed., *Interpreter's Dictionary of the Bible.* 5 vols. Nashville: Abingdon Press, 1962, 1976.

Cully, Iris V., and Cully, Kendig B., *An Introductory Theological Wordbook.* Philadelphia: The Westminster Press, 1964 (youth).

McKenzie, John L., *Dictionary of the Bible*. New York: Macmillan, Inc., 1965.

Richardson, Alan, ed., *Theological Word Book of the Bible*. New York: Macmillan, Inc., 1951.

Bible Concordances

Cruden, Alexander, *Cruden's Compact Concordance*. Grand Rapids, Mich.: The Zondervan Corporation, 1968.

Nelson's Complete Concordance to the Revised Standard Version Bible. Nashville: Thomas Nelson, Inc., 1978.

Strong, James, *Strong's Exhaustive Concordance of the Bible*. Nashville: Broadman Press, 1978.

Young, Robert, *Young's Analytical Concordance to the Bible*. Grand Rapids, Mich.: Wm. B. Eerdmans Publishing Company, 1935.

One-Volume Commentaries

Black, Matthew, and Rowley, H. H., eds., *Peake's Commentary on the Bible*. Nashville: Thomas Nelson, Inc., 1962.

Brown, Raymond et al., *Jerome Biblical Commentary*. Englewood Cliffs, N.J.: Prentice-Hall, Inc., 1969.

Laymon, Charles H., ed., *The Interpreter's One-Volume Commentary on the Bible*. Nashville: Abingdon Press, 1971.

Multi-Volume Commentaries

Cambridge Bible Commentary on the N. E. B. 1968 to present.

The Interpreter's Bible, 12 volumes. Nashville: Abingdon Press.

Other Aids

Brueggemann, Walter, *Living Toward a Vision*. New York: Pilgrim Press, 1976.

Hammer, Paul L., *The Gift of Shalom*. New York: Pilgrim Press, 1976.

White, Hugh C., *Shalom in the Old Testament*. New York: United Church Press (pamphlet).

SESSION 2—BACKGROUND READING

There is no unanimity among North Americans as to what justice is or how we are to achieve it. But we, as Christians, have the Bible and centuries of tradition to guide us in the search for a perspective on justice and for ways to realize it. *Biblical study helps us to discover how the Scriptures serve as a major source of our standards and values.* We have already seen that God's covenant relationship with the Israelites both liberated them and put upon them the obligation to deal justly and generously with one another. In modern society as in biblical times, an obligation is on those in the community of faith to seek justice for the poor, powerless, guilty or innocent.

But there is more to justice than this. Also contained within the word is the notion of a right ordering of relationships. If this harmonious arrangement exists, it will show its presence in a prevailing peace, in social harmony. One Hebrew word that translates best as justice is *tsedeqah*. Also often translated as righteousness, *tsedeqah* encompasses a concern for both fair distribution of goods and for the peace that is the measure of a just society. The prophets many times expressed their concern that *tsedeqah*—a standard for justice or for wholeness in community—required in Yahweh's covenant with Israel was being violated especially in the exploitation of the poor by the wealthy (Amos 5:7; 2:6). They railed particularly against those who did not keep justice "in the gate" because that was where the poor had their only chance of finding relief (Amos 5:12; Isaiah 11:4).

In our day, reflection on justice leads more often to reflection on the "criminal" and on the disruptive effect law breaking has upon our lives and institutions. Few would claim, however, that our efforts to combat crime are moving us at all toward restoring harmony and peace to our communities. Deterrence and rehabilitation may be the expressed aims of the criminal justice system, but the results of its intervention are quite different.

Ray Shonholtz, of the Community Board Project in San Francisco, describes the effects of present intervention efforts in this way:

> the victim receives no restitution or satisfaction; the community or school, which is a real party victim, is not improved or made whole; and, the offender who from a psychological, social or economic perspective may be a victim as well, is given no constructive help in resolving the conflicts that generated the incident in the first place.[1]

[1] Ray Shonholtz, "A Justice System That Isn't Working and Its Impact on the Community" (San Francisco: Community Board, 1978), p. 7.

Justice As Wholeness

Many prison officials have admitted that their institutions are failures except as places for the temporary removal of those few who must be restrained because they represent a danger to themselves or to others. Most persons involved with operating jails and prisons would acknowledge that the inherent isolation and dehumanization, along with the more brutal aspects of some institutions, contribute to returning to society a person less able than ever to live in harmony and peace with his or her community.

If current criminal justice practice is failing at the most practical level as well as when measured against the demands of *tsedeqah*, why does it continue on its same paths? Why do we call for more of the same— more firepower for police, longer prison sentences, and, in some states, a reinstitution of the death penalty? If a frightening medical problem of growing dimensions faced society, we would not pour money and energy into research and treatments that have failed. Why do we persist with an obviously bankrupt approach to crime?

Many advocates of the criminal justice system as it now operates would respond that it is not sustained by the need to punish, nor by the intent to make scapegoats of the convicted few. Rather, they might say, our system has to do with the very biblical idea of retribution, of giving back in proportion to the offense. The *lex talionis*—calling for "an eye for an eye"—is one of the most frequently quoted lines of Scripture (Exodus 21:24) often cited at this point. What those quoting it usually ignore is that the intention of the passage was to place limits on what might be demanded—that is to say, no more than an "eye for an eye." Yet even this limited conception of retribution was refined in time by Jewish theologians and by Jesus, who forgave offenders while demanding only that they go and sin no more.

Further, it is not accurate to translate the Hebrew word *shalam* as "retribution." When *shalam* appears in the Old Testament, "restitution" or "reparation" are more appropriate translations because the word is from the same root as the word that describes the state of a community marked by justice/righteousness, *shalom*. Theologian Kenneth Cauthen draws a useful analogy when he writes of justice as "organic wholeness," pointing out that the community cannot be whole unless each individual within it is sustained by and sustains the others.[2]

[2] Kenneth Cauthen, "Ecojustice and the Future," an address to the American Baptist Churches, U.S.A., 1975, p. 11.

If traditional approaches to doing justice in criminal cases are ruled out as either ineffective or inappropriate from a Christian perspective, how then are we to respond to crime? The answer must lie in new ways of seeking justice. The mechanisms of the state have not shown themselves up to the task; so the community must come forward to take responsibility for resolving conflict.

This is less radical than it may sound. According to Herman Bianchi, law professor and historian at the Free University in Amsterdam:

> In antiquity, in Greek, Hebrew, Roman and Germanic law, state-control took place only in case of evidently important political matters. In all other cases of crime, the members of the community devised a legal system which allowed them to regulate the conflict themselves.
>
> . . . The introduction of state monopoly of crime control and imprisonment by the end of the eighteenth century coincided with the Industrial Revolution and the introduction of total and unconditioned economic liberty. The members of the established power elite (like any other power elite in any other cultural system) needed a system of crime control that would leave their socioeconomic activities outside the scope of crime controls.[3]

The emphasis was on "making right," insofar as possible, whatever wrong had been committed. The victim, often virtually ignored when our system deals with offenders, was usually at the heart of these earlier structures. As for the offender, he or she might be dealt with firmly, but the intent was to restore relations as nearly as possible to the way they were before the disruption. If restitution was possible, that was demanded.

To point in different directions, to suggest the creation of community-centered structures to deal with crime is a beginning which can be made by the religious community. Those directions are superior to any reworking of our present unsuccessful responses to crime in which guilt fixing and punishment take precedence over peaceful and effective resolution of disputes.

Community-centered structures would acknowledge the mandate to work for *tsedeqah,* for the justice that results in *shalom,* the peace and harmony of the community. *Since God's covenant relationship is with all persons, we cannot be in full community with God unless we identify with and seek the fulfillment of all persons.*

Notes on Scripture

Session 2 is based on Isaiah 32:15-20, a passage in which both *tsedeqah* and *shalom* are key words:

[3] Herman Bianchi, "Returning Conflict to the Community—The Alternative of Privatization," U.S. Lecture Tour, 1978.

v. 15. until the Spirit is poured upon us from on high,
and the wilderness becomes a fruitful field,
and the fruitful field is deemed a forest.

v. 16. Then *mishpat* will dwell in the wilderness,
and *tsedeqah* abide in the fruitful field.

v. 17. And the effect of *tsedeqah* will be *shalom,* and
the result of *tsedeqah,* quietness and trust for
ever.

—Isaiah 32:15-17

As the result of a word study on *tsedeqah,* we found it to encompass concern both for fair distribution of goods and for peace. *Tsedeqah* was a concept often used by the prophet Isaiah as a measure of justice or wholeness in the community. The use of this measure or fair distribution and peace sheds light on the prophetic office—which is oftentimes misunderstood.

The Prophetic Office: Obviously, the most apparent definition of a prophet is a person who delivers *prophecy.* Many persons hold misconceptions of prophets because they think prophecy somehow has to predict events or foretell the future. However, prophets are persons who *speak for God!* This speech, directed to a follower of God, suggests what acts should be accomplished or abolished in light of God's will. The word of the prophet is spoken to specific occasions in the life of the community. R. B. Y. Scott in his book *The Relevance of the Prophets* describes the role of prophets in the following manner:

> The prophets of Israel were thus no mere prognosticators; they were spokesmen of a living Word from God. Their frequent references to the future, and especially to the immediate future, result from their sense of the spiritual importance and moral urgency of the present. They were certain of what Yahweh was about to do because of that present situation, which included not only men's attitudes but the fact of God's presence. They spoke in the atmosphere of moments which were critical for Israel because Yahweh's righteous will was present, and his claims were pressing.[4]

Isaiah lived during revolutionary times. John Bright and Bernhard Anderson offer descriptions of those times as well as of Isaiah's response.[5]

[4] R. B. Y. Scott, *The Relevance of the Prophets* (New York: Macmillan, Inc., 1961), pp, 13-17. An excellent book about the role of the prophet in Israel.

[5] John Bright, *A History of Israel* (Philadelphia: The Westminster Press, 1959), p. 288; Bernhard Anderson, *Understanding the Old Testament,* 2nd ed. (Englewood Cliffs: Prentice Hall, Inc., 1966), pp. 300-315.

SESSION 3—What Is Crime? Who Is a Criminal?

SCRIPTURE: John 8:1-11

TIME: 45 minutes to 1 hour

OBJECTIVES

1. To explore the values and attitudes which we hold about crime.
2. To explore differing approaches to behavioral change.
3. To examine both of these from the perspective of our Judeo-Christian heritage.

LEADER PREPARATION

Newsprint, markers, masking tape
Copies of John 8:1-11; Luke 21:38 in the *New English Bible* translation

Advance Preparation

1. Prepare Newsprint Chart 1 for posting at beginning of the session.

SESSION AT A GLANCE

Attitudes About Crime: Word Association and Total Group Sharing	15 minutes
Responses to Lawbreakers	25 minutes
Session Summary	5 minutes

---

2. Prepare Newsprint Charts 2 and 3. See the examples in the Session Outline.
3. Duplicate Handout 1.
4. If session is longer than 45 minutes, prepare Newsprint Chart 4. See the example given.
5. Readings in *Shalom in the Old Testament* by Hugh C. White would be helpful (New York: United Church Press).

SESSION OUTLINE

Begin by reviewing the "Session at a Glance" agenda and timing.

Word Association and Total Group Sharing (15 minutes)

Attitudes About Crime—State that we have all been conditioned to hold negative attitudes about certain kinds of behavior and toward the persons who act out those behaviors. Because crime is a problem in our society and because criminal justice systems are so powerful and so costly, it is particularly important that we examine what preconceived notions we hold about crime and our responses to it.

Explain to members of the group that you want them to call out word associations (the first reaction or feeling that comes to their minds) for each of the acts listed on Newsprint Chart 2 (see box). Record no more than ten associations for each act and allow no more than 5 minutes for this exercise.

ACTS
WORD ASSOCIATIONS

Mugging _____
Employee theft _____
Tax evasion _____
Prostitution _____
Shoplifting _____
Welfare fraud _____
Failure to enforce safety standards _____

Engage the participants in reflection on the list. Allow 8 minutes for total group discussion on the following questions:

1. Look at the list we've developed. Do you see any striking consistencies or inconsistencies in the words we chose?

2. What do the "consistencies" or "inconsistencies" tell us concerning how we feel about these acts?

3. Of those who commit the acts we have listed, who is society most likely to punish? How? Why?

A general view of the Criminal Justice System

This chart seeks to present a simple yet comprehensive view of the movement of cases through the criminal justice system. Procedures in individual jurisdictions may vary from the pattern shown here. The differing weights of line indicate the relative volumes of cases disposed of at various points in the system, but this is only suggestive since no nationwide data of this sort exists.

from the President's Commission on Law Enforcement and the Administration of Justice, "The Challenge of Crime in a Free Society," U. S. Government Printing Office, pp. 8-9. Cited in "A Commission Report: State-local Relations in the Criminal Justice System," 1971, pp. 68-69.

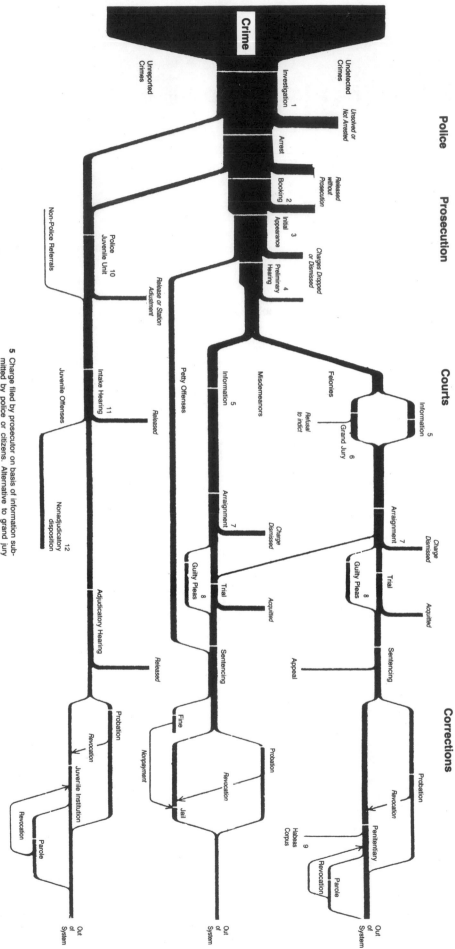

Police   **Prosecution**   **Courts**   **Corrections**

1 May continue until trial.

2 Administrative record of arrest. First step at which temporary release on bail may be available.

3 Before magistrate, commissioner, or justice of peace. Formal notice of charge, advice of rights. Bail set. Summary trials for petty offenses usually conducted here without further processing.

4 Preliminary testing of evidence against defendant. Charge may be reduced. No separate preliminary hearing for misdemeanors in some systems.

5 Charge filed by prosecutor on basis of information submitted by police or citizens. Alternative to grand jury indictment; often used in felonies, almost always in misdemeanors.

6 Reviews whether Government evidence sufficient to justify trial. Some States have no grand jury system; others seldom use it.

7 Appearance for plea; defendant elects trial by judge or jury (if available); counsel for indigent usually appointed here in felonies. Often not at all in other cases.

8 Charge may be reduced at any time prior to trial in return for plea of guilty or for other reasons.

9 Challenge on constitutional grounds to legality of detention. May be sought at any point in process.

10 Police often hold informal hearings, dismiss or adjust many cases without further processing.

11 Probation officer decides desirability of further court action.

12 Welfare agency, social services, counseling, medical care, etc., for cases where adjudicatory handling not needed.

In a summary of this exercise (3 minutes), help participants to see that—

● their responses are tied to some fundamental values and feelings that they hold;

● there will be disagreements in the group about what is a crime, who is a criminal, and what our responses to problem behavior should be;

● the variety of responses indicates a need continually to examine our own attitudes and the laws we support which label people as criminals and result in punishment.

Responses to Lawbreakers (25 minutes)

Ask the participants to gather in groups of three to five persons.

State that we know that laws and attitudes change. So do criminal justice procedures. Thus, unexamined practices may become inconsistent with our values. For the Christian, one of the measures of value is Scripture.

One biblical model of a response to lawbreakers is found in John 8:1-11. Distribute copies of the Bible passage or have someone read it aloud.

Post Newsprint Chart 3, "Responses to Lawbreakers."

RESPONSES TO LAWBREAKERS

1. Since the law prohibited adultery, was the woman a criminal?

2. Did Jesus punish the adulteress? Why? Why not?

3. Would the Pharisees have punished her? Why? Why not?

4. Do you think behavior can be changed without punishment?

Allow at least 15 minutes for small-group discussion of the questions. Then engage the total group in sharing reactions—insights or questions—for the remaining 10 minutes.

Session Summary (5 minutes)

If participants have not reassembled as a group, ask them to do so.*

Distribute Handout 1 by Carlisle Dickson, "What is a crime? Who is a criminal?" Summarize the session by reading the last three paragraphs.

Indicate that, in preparation for the next session, participants should reflect on the purpose of law in society, what motivates us to obey law, and the relationship between law and justice.

*If your session is more than 45 minutes, post Newsprint Chart 4, "Purpose of the Criminal Justice System," and record key points of the participants' discussion of the two questions.

PURPOSE OF THE CRIMINAL JUSTICE SYSTEM

What purpose does our criminal justice system have?	What purpose do we want it to have?

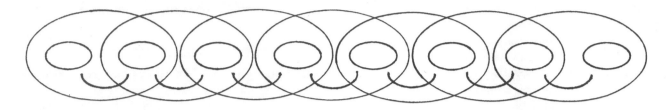

WHAT IS A CRIME? . . .
WHO IS A CRIMINAL?

By CARLISLE H. DICKSON

JOHN DEAN III, a classmate of mine at college, recently spent time in confinement at Ft. Hollabird in Maryland. President Nixon, an unindicted co-conspirator whose taped voice has advocated obstruction of justice, has not been indicted or convicted of any crime.

The question of what is a crime is not always an easy question to answer. Certainly the matter of who is guilty of a crime is also complex.

As children, many of us were taught to be wary of certain types, races, or groups of persons. It is my guess that many of us still have the remnants of those stereotypes embeded within us.

A criminologist by the name of Lambroso, back in the 1800's, was positive that he could identify the pure criminal type ("born that way") and predict criminality by certain physical features (which, of course, Lambroso did not himself possess). Features like an excessive amount of body hair, long ear lobes, slanting forehead, etc., were part of his overall stereotype.

A similar philosophical question has annoyed philosophers over the centuries. Question: If a tree falls in the forest when no one is around to hear, did it make a noise when it fell. Answer: If "noise" is defined as certain sonic vibrations which enter the human ear and thereby produce sound or noise, then no, no noise was made. There was no human there and, therefore, the definition is not met.

RECENT STUDIES by the U.S. Department of Justice suggest that, for certain crime categories, one crime is reported for every three

that are committed. Is it a crime if it is never reported?

What about if it is never noticed? If a bank employe embezzles $3,000 over a period of two years and then over the next two years replaces the money so that his or her employer never discovers the loss, was there a crime? That depends on your definition.

A criminal, except by limiting definitions, doesn't look like anyone you can pick out of a crowd. He (or she) looks very much like most of you who are reading this (but never resembles "me" in the slightest).

It might be said that a criminal can be defined in three ways. First, by the person's self-assessment, regardless of whether or not he or she is caught, convicted, etc. If the person justifies his or her action, one's self-definition is not the label of "criminal."

Second, by the assessments of other people. Was Jesus of Nazareth a criminal? The facts are plain that he was accused, tried, and executed under Roman law for treason. But, most Christians are astounded even to think of Jesus as a criminal.

The third way that a person can be identified as a criminal is by the actions of the criminal justice process (and its reporting in the newspapers). The police are convinced that a person is a criminal if he is arrested; police do not arrest a man or woman whom they do not believe to be guilty.

A Grand Jury indicts those whom they and the District Attorney believe to be guilty. But, what if a jury returns a "not guilty" verdict thereby stating that the evidence was

not sufficient to prove beyond a reasonable doubt that this person did meet the law's definition of guilt for a specific crime? Is that person now or was that person before a criminal?

By the laws legislators pass, by the way those laws are enforced, by the public opinion of the newspapers and community leaders, by all these acting together and in conflict with each other, "society" determines who are the good guys and who are the bad guys.

It is not always a rational process. Historically, there have been strong biases against the members of certain groups who were more easily labelled "criminal" than other group members.

Times change. Laws change. Enforcement procedures change. Sentences to convicted offenders often vary greatly. Public sentiments change. Power balances shift. All these are reflected in the official and the unofficial determinations of what is a crime and who is a criminal.

From *Democrat and Chronicle,* Rochester, New York, January, 1975.
(Mr. Dickson is the Associate Director of the Criminal Justice Training Center at the University of Wisconsin, Milwaukee, and is also an ordained Presbyterian minister. In 1976 he developed the model one-week curriculum for training Wisconsin law enforcement officers in crisis intervention skills, including mediation. Previously, he has been on the staff of the Rochester-Monroe County [N.Y.] Criminal Justice Pilot City Program and the New York State Drug Abuse Control Commission's Division of Prevention.)

SESSION 3—BACKGROUND READING

What is a crime? Who is a criminal?

"I wish," said syndicated Columnist Sydney Harris, "the public would learn to stop using the word 'crime' as a composite word."[1] It is useful, Harris thinks, to divide the acts we now call crime into at least five categories:

Organized crime. This is the highest level of crime in America, penetrating into the very bowels of the civic and political machinery. The social cost of this kind of crime is incalculable, amounting to billions annually.

Sociopathic Crime. This is the crime committed by people who are not psychotic in any clinical sense, but who are products of social conditions—such as relative poverty in a time of affluence, of broken families, drunkenness, child neglect, poor schools, scant community services, and, above all, the sense of alienation and powerlessness in a world too large, too complicated, and too impersonal to cope with.

Psychopathic Crime. This includes a small percentage of persons who commit crimes of impulse or dementia. About 70 percent of all murders are committed by such persons. Most have not engaged in any previous criminal activity and most are not strangers to their victims.

Victimless Crime. These are persons who deviate from the community's norm—gamblers, prostitutes, drug users, drunkards, homosexuals, peddlers of pornographic material, or perhaps merchants who keep their shops open on Sundays.

White Collar Crime. This includes those who fix prices, cheat on income taxes, bribe officials, and employees who steal from their employers.[2]

The list could be extended to include "Official Crime." Since the phenomenon of Watergate in this country, we are all more aware of violations of public trust, perjury committed by elected or appointed officials, and excesses in the granting of immunity. Included in the category of official crimes are the war crimes on which international tribunals and military panels have ruled. Included also are the bribe taking and falsified accounts on which grand juries have brought indictments. As new problems or new consciousness rises, we have other difficult decisions to make: Is war itself a crime? How can a citizenry permit its own government to experiment with germ warfare, using the populace as guinea pigs? Should FBI and CIA personnel be prosecuted for engaging in "dirty tricks" and for alleged roles in assassinations? How should we confront officials who knowingly fail to enforce safety regulations?

The first insight to be gained from listing and categorizing types of crime is that *the problems we face are too complex to be resolved by calls for "more law and order" directed at "street crimes."* The problem is not simplistic nor amenable to any of the panaceas in which Americans are prone to believe. Further, as Sydney Harris points out, we need to make distinctions between widely varying acts in order to come to grips with any of them.

A second insight is that *class and race biases influence the way we view "crime" and "criminals."* Embezzlement, shoplifting, tax evasion, and welfare fraud are all forms of theft. Most people tend to have a higher tolerance for tax evasion than for welfare fraud. Yet, because more people pay taxes than receive welfare, more have certainly been tempted and have undoubtedly succumbed to the temptation to evade taxes than to defraud welfare. The rich have opportunities to embezzle funds, and it is important to keep in mind that "banks and savings and loan associations [lose] more than five and one-half times as much money by embezzlement and fraud as by robbery."[3]

No social or economic class is disproportionately represented in crime committed, but among those who are arrested, prosecuted, sentenced, and imprisoned, the socially underprivileged are unquestionably overrepresented.

William G. Nagel and Jack H. Nagel have researched race and crime correlations. Their major finding is that "There is no significant correlation between a state's racial composition and its crime rate but there is a very great positive relationship between its *racial composition* and its *incarceration* rate."[4]

A third insight is that *the very definition of crime is culturally influenced. The category of "victimless crimes" is particularly subject to the dictates of culture.* It is particularly difficult to achieve consensus on encoding

---

[1]Sydney Harris, "Crime: Three Categories," *Democrat and Chronicle,* Rochester, N.Y., Nov. 7, 1972.

[2]Sydney Harris, adapted from an address to the Bail Fund, Rochester, New York, April 23, 1973. Permission granted.

[3]L. Harold DeWolf, *What Americans Should Do About Crime* (New York: Harper & Row, Publishers, 1976), p. 8. Copyright © 1976 by L. Harold DeWolf. Reprinted by permission of Harper & Row, Publishers, Inc.

[4]William G. Nagel, "On Behalf of a Moratorium on Prison Construction," *Crime and Delinquency,* April, 1977; and Jack H. Nagel, "Crime and Incarceration: A Reanalysis," School of Public and Urban Policy, University of Pennsylvania, September, 1978.

or enforcing laws about gambling, use of drugs (alcohol being the most common), sexual relations, or Sunday sales in retail stores. The drive to repeal prohibition laws is the classic example of the dilemma posed when we try to "legislate morality."

The conclusion we must reach is one which both quipsters and analysts have stated: "The major cause of crime is law." By the same token, the causes of anti-social or violent behavior are extremely complex and resist resolution through legal processes alone.

The reason that we write criminal codes is to define the conditions under which the citizenry wants the state to intervene in the lives of individuals, in corporate affairs, or in official functions. Because tremendous coercive power accompanies state intervention, we should approach with extreme caution and with vigilant monitoring the granting of that power. Additionally, laws which exist but are not enforced lead to cynicism about the legal process. It behooves, then, those who write criminal laws to "know what they want" and "when there is the will to enforce" criminal codes.

The reality human beings must face is that we all—rich and poor alike—are tempted and all give in occasionally in spite of our good intentions and God's grace. Even Paul admitted, "For I do not do the good I want, but the evil I do not want is what I do" (Romans 7:19).

The question we must raise is about how to respond to those of us who succumb to temptation. There is no real advantage and, indeed, there are many apparent disadvantages to labeling problematic behavior as "crime" and those who exhibit the behavior as "criminal."

Our society is complex and our responses have become depersonalized. The responses of societies we tend to label primitive may help us in pursuit of answers to our question. L. Harold DeWolf writes of the response of the Shona-speaking people in Zimbabwe (Rhodesia):

> When a man in such a village steals, assaults, or otherwise injures another, the subchief or headman must first find out who committed the crime. After that, his attention is directed to working out a plan for restitution, as well as possible, to the victim, victims, or next of kin. Eventually the offender and his family must give to the headman part or all the food for a community feast to celebrate the conclusion of the affair. The victim(s) will have received cattle, money, or labor from the offender and his family. At the high point of the feast, the headman will recount to all what has been done. Then he will ask the victim and family, "Are you

satisfied?" They will reply that they are satisfied. Then he will ask the offender and his family whether they are satisfied. They, too, will reply affirmatively. The headman will ask all assembled whether they are satisfied. After their affirmative reply, he will solemnly intone, "Then it is finished." After that the community is whole again and it would be intolerably ill-mannered for anyone ever to mention again the crime that was done.[5]

There are direct parallels between this tribal model and the concept of justice as wholeness (*tsedeqah*). There are direct parallels also with Jesus' approaches to the lawbreakers of his day. Session 3 encourages examination of a specific response by Jesus—to the adulteress who was in danger of being stoned by the scribes and Pharisees for her "crime."

Notes on Scripture

In this section we shall explore an aspect of "detailed studies of a particular text" (see Introduction) which is pertinent to the passage about Jesus and the adulteress (John 8:1-11).

When one looks up John 8:1-11 in the *Oxford Annotated Bible,* one notices immediately the use of small print and footnotes. The reason for singling out this particular passage is related to studies of its use in earlier manuscripts.

Research attempting to locate the earliest and most historically authentic manuscripts of New Testament sources is called "textual criticism." Since the Gospels and Pauline letters have been copied so many times throughout history, distortions are discovered in the texts. For instance, some ancient authorities place John 8:1-11 in John 7:53–8:11, but in other ancient manuscripts John 8:1-11 is found in John 21:24ff., and in other manuscripts it is found in Luke 21:39ff.[6] While this exercise in textual criticism can be very technical, it is useful to be aware of it as a tool for determining how different New Testament authors and editors placed texts according to the importance they placed upon a particular aspect of the ministry of Jesus; then, how that ministry was interpreted in the early church and to each succeeding generation.

[5]DeWolf, *op.cit.,* p. 105.
[6]Kurt Aland, ed., *The Greek New Testament* , 2nd ed. (Stuttgart, West Germany: Württemberg Bible Society, 1966, 1968), pp. 355 and 413, footnotes.

SESSION 4—Law and Justice

SCRIPTURE: Matthew 18:23-35

TIME: 45 minutes to 1 hour

OBJECTIVE

To explore with participants the reasons for adhering to law, the purpose of law in society, and the relationship between law and justice.

LEADER PREPARATION

Materials needed:

Newsprint, felt-tip pens, markers

Advance Preparation

1. Prepare Newsprint Chart 1 for posting at the beginning of the session.

```
┌─────────────────────────────────────────┐
│         SESSION AT A GLANCE               │
│  Learning Centers          15 minutes     │
│  Guided Discussion         25 minutes     │
│  Session Summary            5 minutes     │
└─────────────────────────────────────────┘
```

2. Prepare Newsprint Chart 2 on "Stages of Moral Development" for posting at the appropriate time.

3. Prepare posters for the four Learning Centers by pasting copies of the material labeled #1, #2, #3, and #4 on poster board.

4. Arrange the room so that there are four Learning Centers in each of which you have displayed one of the posters.

5. Make copies of Handouts 1 and 2.

SESSION OUTLINE

As the Session Begins

Review the "Session at a Glance" schedule and timing. Explain that the first activity will involve exploring the relationship of law and justice in each of four Learning Centers.

MORAL DEVELOPMENT/VIEW OF LAW
Stages of Moral Development[1] Where Do the Actors Fit?

Stage 1: Laws are obeyed out of fear of punishment.

Stage 2: Law is obeyed out of desire to please self and others.

Stage 3: "Good" people obey the law.

Stage 4: Society would fall apart if the law weren't obeyed.

Stage 5: Laws are to protect personal liberty, not simply to restrain.

Stage 6: Laws may be broken if they violate principles of justice and dignity.

Learning Centers (15 minutes)

Give each participant an "Opinionnaire," Handout 1. Tell them that they will cover four centers but can start at any one of the four. In Learning Center #1, they will work with the story of Valjean; in #2 with Matthew 18:23-25; in #3 with the Bill of Rights; in #4 with a Safe Driver's Test.

When they have completed the Opinionnaire, they should return to you for Handout 2. Allow no more than 15 minutes for both activities.

Group Discussion (25 minutes)

Have the group assemble for discussion. First, try to elicit responses from the participants about how it felt to do these exercises. Ask if they experienced frustrations in making their choices.

Explain that these exercises are based upon the conflict

[1] See Lawrence Kohlberg, "Stages of Moral Development as a Basis for Moral Education," in *Moral Education,* edited by C. M. Beck, B. S. Crittenden, and E. V. Sullivan (New York: Newman Press, 1971), pp. 23-92.

41

story format devised by Harvard educator and psychologist, Lawrence Kohlberg. Based upon extensive studies in many nations, Kohlberg contends that there are various "stages" of moral development through which most people pass. Some persons become frozen at one stage and cease to develop further. At each stage, there are different beliefs about the nature of law and of justice.[2]

Briefly explain the key points of Kohlberg's stages of moral development and indicate where the possible responses to the four questions on Handout 2 might fall on Newsprint Chart 2. (Use Newsprint Chart 2.)

Learning Center #1, C. Write "tailor" opposite Stage 4 on the newsprint chart. Participants who agreed with Item C that for the tailor not to report Valjean might lead to the breakdown of the laws of society may be thinking at Stage 4—that the only way society can be ordered is through law.

Learning Center #2, B. Write "servant" opposite Stage 2. Participants who agreed that the servant's desperate financial condition justified his having his debtor thrown into prison may be thinking at Stage 2—most concerned about one's own needs or teaching by "tit for tat."

Learning Center #3, A. Write "dissenters" opposite Stage 6. Participants who disagreed with Item A may

[2] *Ibid.*

be thinking at Stage 6—that laws may be broken if they violate principles of justice.

Learning Center #4. Write "Driver A" opposite Stage 5—agreeing to drive within the limit shows concern for the social contract, rights of all.

Write "Driver B" opposite Stage 1—punishment is the only way to correct or deter unsafe drivers.

Write "Driver C" opposite Stage 6—Human life is the ultimate value.

Write "Driver D" opposite Stage 2—Satisfy one's own needs.

Write "Driver E" opposite Stage 4—Laws are needed to maintain order.

Write "Driver F" opposite Stage 3—Desire for approval.

Caution: Indicate that Kohlberg's ranking methods are too complex to unravel in such a brief time. They are introduced here only to cause us to think about why we obey law and what purpose we want law to serve. Allow only the briefest of comments here.

Session Summary (5 minutes)

Ask, "Why do we obey laws?" Responses will probably include ideas from earlier sessions on the nature of justice. If not, try to tie the discussion in with the concept of *tsedeqah* by asking, "At which of Kohlberg's levels is justice best served?"

LEARNING CENTER #1
(to be placed on a poster)

In a country in Europe, a poor man named Valjean could find no work nor could his sister and brother. Without money, he stole food and medicine that they needed. He was captured and sentenced to prison for six years. After a couple of years, he escaped from the prison and went to live in another part of the country under a new name. He saved money and slowly built up a big factory. He gave his workers the highest wages and used most of his profits to build a hospital for people who couldn't afford good medical care. Twenty years had passed when a tailor recognized the factory owner as being Valjean, the escaped convict whom the police had been looking for back in his hometown.

LEARNING CENTER #2
(to be placed on a poster)

"Therefore the kingdom of heaven may be compared to a king who wished to settle accounts with his servants.

When he began the reckoning, one was brought to him who owed him ten thousand talents;

and as he could not pay, his lord ordered him to be sold, with his wife and children and all that he had, and payment to be made.

So the servant fell on his knees, imploring him, 'Lord, have patience with me, and I will pay you everything.'

And out of pity for him the lord of that servant released him and forgave him the debt.

But that same servant, as he went out, came upon one of his fellow servants who owed him a hundred denarii; and seizing him by the throat he said, 'Pay what you owe.'

So his fellow servant fell down and besought him, 'Have patience with me, and I will pay you.'

He refused and went and put him in prison till he should pay the debt.

When his fellow servants saw what had taken place, they were greatly distressed, and they went and reported to their lord all that had taken place.

Then his lord summoned him and said to him, 'You wicked servant! I forgave you all that debt because you besought me;

and should not you have had mercy on your fellow servant, as I had mercy on you?'

And in anger his lord delivered him to the jailers, till he should pay all his debt.

So also my heavenly Father will do to every one of you, if you do not forgive your brother from your heart" (Matthew 18:23-35).

LEARNING CENTER #3
(to be placed on a poster)

AMENDMENTS TO THE CONSTITUTION

ARTICLES I-X (THE BILL OF RIGHTS), 1791

Article I

Congress shall make no law respecting an establishment of religion, or prohibiting the free exercise thereof; or abridging the freedom of speech, or of the press; or the right of the people peaceably to assemble, and to petition the Government for a redress of grievances.

Article II

A well-regulated Militia, being necessary to the security of a free State, the right of the people to keep and bear Arms, shall not be infringed.

Article III

No Soldier shall, in time of peace be quartered in any house, without the consent of the Owner, nor in time of war, but in a manner to be prescribed by law.

Article IV

The right of the people to be secure in their persons, houses, papers, and effects, against unreasonable searches and seizures, shall not be violated, and no Warrants shall issue, but upon probable cause, supported by Oath or affirmation, and particularly describing the place to be searched, and the persons or things to be seized.

Article V

No person shall be held to answer for a capital, or otherwise infamous crime, unless on a presentment or indictment of a Grand Jury, except in cases arising in the land or naval forces, or in the Militia, when in actual service in time of War or public danger; nor shall any person be subject for the same offence to be twice put in jeopardy of life or limb; nor shall be compelled in any criminal case to be a witness against himself, nor

be deprived of life, liberty, or property, without due process of law; nor shall private property be taken for public use, without just compensation.

Article VI

In all criminal prosecutions, the accused shall enjoy the right to a speedy and public trial, by an impartial jury of the State and district wherein the crime shall have been committed, which district shall have been previously ascertained by law, and to be informed of the nature and cause of the accusation; to be confronted with the witnesses against him; to have compulsory process for obtaining witnesses in his favor, and to have the Assistance of Counsel for his defense.

Article VII

In Suits at Common law, where the value in controversy shall exceed twenty dollars, the right of trial by jury shall be preserved, and no fact tried by a jury, shall be otherwise re-examined in any Court of the United States, than according to the rules of the common law.

Article VIII

Excessive bail shall not be required, nor excessive fines imposed, nor cruel and unusual punishments inflicted.

Article IX

The enumeration in the Constitution, of certain rights, shall not be construed to deny or disparage others retained by the people.

Article X

The powers not delegated to the United States by the Constitution, nor prohibited by it to the States, are reserved to the States respectively, or to the people.

LEARNING CENTER #4
(to be placed on a poster)

"Come now, let us reason together, says the Lord:
though your sins are like scarlet,
they shall be as white as snow;
though they are red like crimson,
they shall become like wool."

—Isaiah 1:18

The psychologist Lawrence Kohlberg, like the prophet Isaiah, contends that each of us is a moral philosopher. Each of us develops rationalizations to explain why we "ought" or "ought not" to do something. In other words, there is a kind of consistency to our personal morality. Sometimes, this is called our "character."

Test your consistency by answering the questions about safe driving on the opinionnaire.

OPINIONNAIRE ON VARIOUS BEHAVIORS

	YES	NO

LEARNING CENTER #1

A. The tailor had an obligation to report Valjean as an escaped convict. ___ ___

B. Because Valjean paid his workers well and built a hospital for poor people, the judge should not send him back to prison. ___ ___

C. Not reporting known criminals such as Valjean could lead to breakdown of the laws of society. ___ ___

LEARNING CENTER #2

A. The master did the right thing in canceling the debt of the servant. ___ ___

B. The servant's desperate financial condition justified his having his debtor thrown into prison. ___ ___

C. The servants who complained to the master would have done better to discuss their disapproval with the unforgiving servant. ___ ___

LEARNING CENTER #3

A. People should not be allowed to congregate in public places for the purpose of dissent. ___ ___

B. Taxpayers should have to pay for lawyers for poor defendants. ___ ___

C. No restrictions should be put on the authority of police to search the property and person of anyone suspected of a crime. ___ ___

LEARNING CENTER #4

A. When you apply for a driver's license, you agree to drive within the speed limit. ___ ___

B. Unsafe drivers should be caught, fined, and jailed. ___ ___

C. Human life is sacred and must be protected by safe driving. ___ ___

D. "Drive safely, the life you save may be your own." ___ ___

E. Good drivers should not exceed posted speed limits. ___ ___

F. "Good drivers drive at safe speeds." ___ ___

STAGES OF MORAL DEVELOPMENT

Adapted from an article entitled "The Child as a Moral Philosopher," by Lawrence Kohlberg, Harvard educator, in *Psychology Today,* September, 1968

Stage 1: "The physical consequences of action . . . determine its goodness or badness." Laws are obeyed out of fear of punishment.

Stage 2: Behavior is based on what satisfies one's needs and on what satisfies the needs of others, if reciprocity is involved—"You scratch my back and I'll scratch yours." Law is accepted without question.

Stage 3: People conform in order to gain approval—"Good people obey the law."

Stage 4: Behavior is based on a "law and order" orientation. Society would fall apart if people didn't do their duty and obey the law.

Stage 5: This is the stage of "social contract." People at this stage emphasize individual rights and civil liberties. Laws are to *protect* personal liberty, not simply to restrain bad behavior. There is an emphasis on majority will.

Stage 6: People at this stage behave according to universal principles, such as justice and the inherent value of human life. Laws may be broken if they violate such principles, or if principles will be enhanced by the breaking of a law.

WHAT IS YOUR ANSWER TO THE FOLLOWING QUESTIONS?

1. *Learning Center #1.* At what stage of moral reasoning would you be if you agreed that the tailor's not reporting Valjean would lead to the breakdown of society?

2. *Learning Center #2.* At what stage would you be if you agreed that the servant was justified in having his debtor thrown into prison?

3. *Learning Center #3.* At what stage would you be if you disagreed that persons should not be allowed to congregate for the purpose of dissent?

4. *Learning Center #4.* At what stage would you be if you agreed with the statement of Driver A? Driver B? Driver C? Driver D? Driver E? Driver F?

SESSION 4—BACKGROUND READING

Law and Justice

The unjust servant (Matthew 18:23-35) did not perceive right and wrong in terms of justice but in terms of advantage for himself. Having just benefited from the king's agreement to set aside the law, the unjust servant wanted to invoke the law in order to collect from his debtor.

One is tempted to be harsh with the unforgiving servant. However, he deserves both sympathy and understanding. The king could afford to be generous: after all, the money owed him was not essential for his livelihood. The servant, on the other hand, had just gone through the harrowing experience of almost being sentenced to prison until his debt was paid. He could ill afford to offer the same generosity as the king. His lack of ready cash had jeopardized not only his own life but the lives of his family as well. We can readily understand his dilemma and his temptation to turn to authorities to press his own case.

However, the difference between the king and the servant and the similarity of the response demanded of both of them is what is remarkable in Jesus' parable. Over and over again in his parables, Jesus made this point: the elements of justice are the same even though the situations may be quite different. If the king was "just" when he responded to the need of the servant, then the servant could be "just" only when he responded in some way to the need of his debtor. If justice could not be done by strict application of the law for the servant, then it also could not be done by strict application to the servant's debtor.

Jesus abhorred legalism. When he came in contact with those whom his society had labeled as "outcasts" or "sinners," he responded to their need. For Jesus, doing justice involved compassion and forgiveness and "making right" the person's situation.

For the person of faith no definition of justice is valid unless it is consistent with God's idea of righteousness—right making. We can only try to emulate the model of Jesus Christ or try to conform to the visions of biblical figures.

So it is with law. The word "law" is used to define several concepts, and we must decide by which laws we will live. There are the physical laws of nature, which are beyond our power to change, such as the law of gravity. There is natural law, God's intention for human beings and the consequent natural rights which human beings possess. With Paul, we believe that God's law is "written on [our] hearts" (Romans 2:15). It is our conscience, a firm base from which we can be guided by the Spirit. With the framers of our Declaration of Independence, we believe that there are certain rights—among them life, liberty, and the pursuit of happiness—which arise from natural law and which must be protected.

In the Old Testament, law *(torah)* "denotes the guidance or *instruction* which comes from God through the oracular utterances of the priests or through the prophets; it is the whole content of God's revelation of his nature and purpose, which incidentally makes clear man's responsibility before God." New Testament writers tended to stress that the *torah* was the "legislation or legal system of a community, in particular of Israel according to the OT." It was their conviction that "the 'grace' and 'truth' which the *torah* was to establish, according to many OT promises, did not come through the legislation attributed to Moses. They came by Jesus Christ who had been condemned as a result of that very legislation." [1] However, when one carefully studies *torah* in the Old Testament tradition, one is sure to find evidences of the "grace" and "truth" which Christ reflected in his ministry. The Old Testament is a part of our Christian Bible because *torah,* rightly understood, is the "Word of God."[2]

The written law can be ecclesiastical or secular. Church law has, at times past, functioned as a legal system, and even heresy trials have been conducted under its statutes. In twentieth-century America, the written secular law is enacted by legislatures, the bodies given that power by the citizenry.

Some people give to the state the power to make law and then assume that to obey law is to do justice. They never distinguish between the two. They forget that if Moses' mother had obeyed the law, her midwife would have disposed of her son at birth (Exodus 1–3). Instead, she broke the law and thus gave her son the chance to become the great lawgiver of Israel. If Daniel had obeyed the law, he would have denied his God. He did neither, and the king of the Medes and the Persians threw him into the lions' den from whence his God saved him (Daniel 6). If the Israelites had obeyed the law, they

---

[1] Alan Richardson, ed., *A Theological Word Book of the Bible* (New York: Macmillan, Inc., 1971), pp. 122-123.
[2] *Ibid.*

would have died in slavery. Instead they obeyed God by setting out across the desert to establish a still vibrant community of faith (Exodus 12).

Those who give to the state the power to make law and then assume that to obey it is to do justice forget that written law, in itself, has no life. It has to be applied and interpreted. When it is applied, it becomes utilitarian—it is screened through the assumption of the judge or the jury, those who for the most part represent the status quo, the same power configurations represented by the legislators who wrote the law. In criminal law, judgment and discretion enter in at every point—whether the police arrest, the district attorney prosecutes, the judge administers sanctions, and whether the probation officer or parole board releases or retains. There is, in actuality, no "positive law," no way strictly to interpret the "letter of the law."

Therefore, religious people accept only God's law as absolute because they know that human laws in their writing and in their application sometimes only approximate God's law and sometimes even contradict it. Believers and unbelievers both should have had problems obeying all the laws of Nazi Germany. Many had a hard time living with their consciences during the hostilities between the United States and Vietnam. These and so many analogous events cause religious people to be aware that God's law is a necessary test for justice in human law.

The purpose of law, then, is to insure the realization of each person's fundamental human rights and to facilitate the doing of justice between persons. To deny that human law is absolute does not mean that law is unnecessary. Every society has rules or laws and either formal or informal systems of enforcing them. When we write laws, we are trying to make provision for the following broad concerns.

First, respect for the rights of each person compels us continually to seek more adequate formulations of laws.

Second, laws should ideally codify the golden rule so that by obeying the law citizens would be "doing to others what they would have others do to them." Our civil laws which deal with the regulation of traffic, drugs, commerce, and family matters and our criminal laws which deal with preventing injury or exploitation are examples of how laws are designed to simplify exchanges between individuals.

Third, laws in both the civil and criminal code protect us against undue intervention on the part of the state into our lives and from undue intervention on the part of one citizen into the life of another. The "due process" built into our Bill of Rights and into our case law restrains the power of the state.

The best protection against the power of the state lies in education of the citizenry. When each citizen is a participating member of the community, the role of law can be limited. Law should always be seen as a means, not an end. Two good maxims of political science are: "resort to law should be as limited as possible" and "laws should be made to serve people; people should not be made to serve the law."

Indeed, *there appears to be a relationship between our reasons for obeying laws and our stages of moral understanding and action.* Harvard educator Lawrence Kohlberg contends that most people in American society believe that to be law-abiding is to be a "good, moral person." Most Americans respect law and believe that law enforcers, lawyers, and judges all share a lofty, almost "sacred" role of seeing to it that law is obeyed.

People with this view believe that law is important because it maintains order within society. Kohlberg believes that they see laws as "necessary to restrain . . . not only physical violence but disregard for authority, for the nation, and for the economic system. . . ." [3] Thus they expect others to be law-abiding; they expect praise for those who support the system defended by law and either punishment or restraint for those who criticize it.

If Kohlberg's analysis is correct, the average American citizen does not ask whether laws are just but only whether certain actions are prohibited or permitted by law. That helps to explain why law and order have been such popular rallying cries in the United States. Unfortunately, it explains, also, how reverence for law and order may coexist with widespread injustice.

That attitude explains how laws which permitted slavery and which denied the right of women to possess property existed for so long; how the amendment to the Constitution which permitted black males to vote still withheld the voting right from all females for forty years; how the Thirteenth Amendment to the Constitution *still* makes provision for penal slavery.

Kohlberg contends, on the other hand, that there are people at higher stages of ethical development who rely on conscience rather than law. Those people believe that they can and should analyze law to see if what it requires conforms to what their consciences indicate is just. Peo-

[3] Lawrence Kohlberg, "Moral Judgment Interview and Procedures for Scoring," Harvard University, Cambridge, Massachusetts, 1971, Issue A.

ple who understand law in this way make poor subjects for tyrants; they make good social change agents; and they are aware that law should not be manipulated for their own advantage.

Like the king in the parable of the unjust servant, people at higher stages of ethical development understand that law must be interpreted, must be put into context, and must sometimes be set aside if justice is to be done.

Session 4 introduces participants to the work of Lawrence Kohlberg as a tool for evaluating the way criminal law influences "justice" in our land. *If members of the religious community will use this and other tools to examine our present ineffective and inhumane responses to crime, it should be possible to suggest responses which are more consistent with the biblical concept of "justice as wholeness."*

The biblical idea of justice is based, above all else, on the idea that a tree has to be judged by its fruits. The fruit of justice, *tsedeqah,* should be peace. Peace, in its biblical sense, means a state of the community where members can really communicate, realize themselves, no one excepted.[4]

Theologian Paul Tillich says that in personal encounters creative justice has three functions: "It is its first task to listen." The second function is giving. "Giving is an expression of creative justice if it serves the purpose of reuniting love." The third function in which love is united with justice is in forgiving. "For it is the only way of reuniting those who are estranged by guilt. Without reconciliation there is no reunion. Forgiving love is the only way of fulfilling the intrinsic claim in every being, namely its claim to be reaccepted into the unity to which it belongs." [5]

Human law and justice are always in tension. Only in God's law are they in unity.

[4] Dr. Herman Bianchi, "Tsedeka-Justice," review for *Philosophy and Theology* (Central Printing Company, Sept., 1973).

[5] Paul Tillich, *Love, Power, and Justice* (New York: Oxford University Press, 1954), pp. 84ff.

SESSION 5—Prisons As a Social Problem

SCRIPTURE: Matthew 7:7-12

TIME: 45 minutes to 1 hour

OBJECTIVES
1. To have participants consider why we continue to rely on prisons.
2. To evaluate whether prisons are compatible with a society based upon *tsedeqah*.

LEADER PREPARATION

Materials needed:
Newsprint, felt-tip pens, masking tape

Advance Preparation

1. Prepare Newsprint Chart 1 for posting at the beginning of the session.

```
SESSION AT A GLANCE
Why Prisons?                          5 minutes
Myths and Realities
(paired discussion)                  10 minutes
Prisons As a Social Problem          20 minutes
Sharing and Session Summary          10 minutes
```

2. Duplicate Handout 1, "Myths and Realities," so that each participant can be given a role during the paired discussions.

3. Duplicate Handouts 2 and 3.

4. Prepare Newsprint Charts 2 and 3 as shown in the Session Outline.

SESSION OUTLINE

As the Session Begins

Review the "Session at a Glance" agenda and schedule with the participants.

Why Prisons? (5 minutes)

Post Newsprint Chart 2, "Why Do We Put People in Prisons?" Ask participants to call out all the reasons they can name. Record their responses and leave them posted.

```
WHY DO WE PUT PEOPLE IN PRISONS?
```

Myths and Realities About Prisons (10 minutes)

Tell the participants that we all know that misconceptions about prisons are common. We hear them in everyday conversation. Most people think that prisons are necessary to protect us; yet we continue to experience crime.

Ask that the participants form discussion pairs (each person should try to pair with another member of the group whom he or she does not know well). Tell them that they are going to engage in a "street-corner conversation" with an "old friend" with whom the subject of a new prison comes up.

Give every person a role card (one member of the discussion pair a "myth"; the other its "reality"). Tell participants to take one minute to develop their argument. After one minute ask them to begin their discussion with their "friend." Allow four minutes for the discussion to occur.

For five minutes engage the total group in reacting to the questions on Newsprint Chart 3.

```
QUESTIONS FOR DISCUSSION
1) Which argument was easier to develop?
2) Which was more convincing?
3) How did your discussion differ from our an-
   swers to "Why do we put people in prisons?"
```

Prisons As a Social Problem (20 minutes)

Give each participant Handout 2, with "Prisons As a Social Problem" and Bible passages. Ask participants to spend the next 20 minutes (in groups of four) discussing whether we should continue to use and expand our prison system, and to be prepared to share their conclusions with the total group. Give 5- minute and 2-minute notices as the time to conclude discussion approaches.

Sharing and Session Summary (10 minutes)

After each group has shared a summary of its discussion, point out that "since prisons are becoming rec-ognized as a problem in themselves, the remaining sessions will emphasize alternatives for a safer society" and that each person should be envisioning or finding references to alternatives to prisons.

While imprisonment began as a humane alternative to other forms of punishment for wrongdoers—such as branding an adulteress or cutting off the hand of a thief—two hundred years of living with this uniquely American "experiment" have shown it to be a colossal failure. It is important for us to examine *why* we continue to rely upon it, and to ask ourselves if a society which values justice might not be more imaginative in its approaches to the conflicts we now call crimes. Are there feasible alternatives to imprisonment?

MYTHS AND REALITIES

(Duplicate and cut the copies into role cards for the
paired discussions.)

MYTH: Prisons rehabilitate. Putting persons in prison represents a humane advance over methods which included public floggings, brandings, and mutilation. Those who habitually break the law need to be isolated so they can ponder their misdeeds (in fact, that's where the term "penitentiary" came from). As children need to be "corrected" when they misbehave, adults need to be punished. Treatment programs are available, also.

MYTH: The United States uses prisons much less frequently than other industrialized nations. Apparently we don't use them often enough since we have the highest rate of violent crime among all Western democracies. U.S. males (white) commit three times as many homicides as males of all races in Canada; ten times as many as males in the Netherlands or Scandinavia.

MYTH: All persons who are in prison pose a serious threat to society and require maximum security. One of the reasons for our high rate of crime is that judges don't send enough law violators to prison.

MYTH: All persons behind bars have been sentenced. They may not *all* have been sentenced yet, but they must have done something wrong or they wouldn't be there.

MYTH: All social classes and ethnic groups are proportionately represented in prisons. If some groups are overrepresented in prison, it must be because they commit more crimes than do other groups. If we don't put lawbreakers in prison, society eventually will fall apart.

REALITY: There is nearly universal agreement that prisons *do not rehabilitate* those who must spend time in them. Of those who are in prison 70 percent have been there before (*Time* magazine, June 30, 1975). Frequently, when a person leaves prison, that person is more embittered against society than when he or she entered. Prisons have been called "graduate schools for crime."

REALITY: The United States imprisons more persons than any of the other Western industrialized nations. Holland, for example, imprisons 22 persons per 100,000 population; the United States imprisons 250 persons per 100,000. Most states and the federal government are expanding prisons. Apparently putting people in prison has not made us safer.

REALITY: Many wardens maintain that less than 15 percent of those in prison require maximum security. The number who require maximal restraint may be as low as 1 percent.

REALITY: Over one-half of those in local jails are not sentenced. They are awaiting disposition or sentencing. Many are in jail less than two days, innocent until proven guilty.

REALITY: Poor persons and members of minority groups are overrepresented in prison, compared to their ratio in society. We are very selective about whom we imprison. Racial minorities constitute 15 percent of the United States' population; 44 percent of prison populations. In New York State, minorities account for 72 percent of prison populations.

PRISONS AS A SOCIAL PROBLEM

"Ask, and it will be given you; seek and you will find; knock, and it will be opened to you. For every one who asks receives, and he who seeks finds, and to him who knocks it will be opened. Or what man of you, if his son asks him for a loaf, will give him a stone? Or if he asks for a fish, will give him a serpent? If you then, who are evil, know how to give good gifts to your children, how much more will your Father who is in heaven give good things to those who ask him! So whatever you wish that men would do to you, do so to them; for this is the law and the prophets" (Matthew 1:7-12).

"It is very important that besides looking at the penal system as a means to solve problems, we should also have another perspective on the system. This other perspective means that *we have to look upon the penal system as a social problem in itself.* If it is true that the output of the system is evil, if the system's impact on the society is as big as I think it is; if the social costs of the system are spread so unevenly over the already existing injustices; then the penal system is a very important social problem. *It is a more important social problem than many of the social problems we are using the penal system to solve."*

Louk H. C. Hulsman, "The Penal System as a Social Problem." Hulsman is on the Faculty of Law, Erasmus University, Rotterdam, the Netherlands. This quote is from a talk given on May 3, 1974, in Racine, Wisconsin.

*In the wilderness justice will come to live
and integrity in the fertile land;
integrity will bring peace,
justice give lasting security.*

*My people will live in a peaceful home,
in safe houses,
in quiet dwellings.*
—*Isaiah 32:16-18 (The Jerusalem Bible)*

Quotations for Reflection

What is often neglected in official statements is not that prisons fail to rehabilitate, but the active nature of destruction that occurs in prison. (California State Assembly Committee on Criminal Procedure, *Deterrent Effects of Criminal Sanctions,* 1966)

In the outside society, unity and a sense of community contribute to personal growth. In the society of prisoners, unity and community must be discouraged lest the many overwhelm the few. In the world outside, leadership is an ultimate virtue. In the world inside, leadership must be identified, isolated, and blunted. . . . Other qualities considered good on the outside—self-confidence, pride, individuality—are eroded by the prison experience into self-doubts, obsequiousness, and lethargy. In short, individuality is obliterated and the spirit of man is broken in the spiritlessness of obedience. (William Nagel, former prison warden and director of The American Foundation and director of its Institute of Corrections, in *The New Red Barn: A Critical Look at the Modern American Prison* [New York: Walker & Company, 1973], p. 139.)

If New York has many, many times the armed robberies of London, if Philadelphia has twoscore the criminal homicides of Vienna, if Chicago has more burglaries than all of Japan, if Los Angeles has more drug addiction than Western Europe, then must we not concentrate on the social and economic ills of New York, Philadelphia, Chicago, Los Angeles, America? That has not been our approach. We concentrate on locking up the offender while we ignore the underlying causes. (Nagel, *op, cit.,* p. 151.)

All efforts consistent with the safety of others should be made to reduce involvement of the individual offender with the institutional aspects of corrections. The alienation and dehumanization engendered in jails, workhouses, prisons, even probation, (are) to be avoided wherever possible. The less penetration into the criminal justice system the better. (National Advisory Commission on Criminal Justice Standards and Goals, *Corrections* (1973), p. 223.)

SESSION 5—BACKGROUND READING

Prisons As a Social Problem

It is not uncommon for prison administrators to admit, even publicly, that today's prisons are a failure. William Nagel, former prison warden and director of the American Foundation, states the case against prisons in his book, *The New Red Barn*:

In the outside society, unity and a sense of community contribute to personal growth. In the society of prisoners, unity and community must be discouraged lest the many overwhelm the few. In the world outside, leadership is an ultimate virtue. In the world inside, leadership must be identified, isolated, and blunted. . . . Other qualities considered good on the outside—self-confidence, pride, individuality—are eroded by the prison experience into self-doubts, obsequiousness, and lethargy. In short, individuality is obliterated and the spirit of man is broken in the spiritlessness of obedience.[1]

If prisons erode positive personal qualities, about all that can be said on behalf of these institutions is that they remove some offenders from society for some period of time. A small percentage of the men and women now imprisoned can be generally agreed to be dangerous to themselves or others. The question we must ask ourselves is: if they must be restrained for safety's sake, how can that occur in a humane and restorative environment?

Well, it may be said, "At least we've caught some and have removed them from the street. Perhaps they and those lawbreakers not yet imprisoned will learn a lesson and 'go straight' in the future." The most basic flaw in that argument is exposed by the rate of recidivism—the number of persons who leave prison only to return. Prisons deserve their label of "graduate schools for crime." On the one hand, the dehumanizing prison experience itself and the stigmatizing effect of prison make it difficult for releasees to "go straight." On the other hand, the first-time offender is coerced by or attracted to the person who, for want of a more satisfying life-style, has adopted "crime" as a way of life.

What then of the stated goals for imprisonment—protection of society, rehabilitation, punishment, and deterrence? Is society safer for having locked up thousands of persons? The answer, quite obviously, is no. Few persons who commit crimes are caught, brought to trial, convicted, and imprisoned. Our prisons are full of tokens of society's impotent rage against crime. The human and fiscal costs of maintaining prisons as we know them are enormous and not worth the price of restraining the few who can be reasonably identified as "dangerous."

The deterrence argument breaks down when we realize that lawbreakers, for the most part, fit into one of three categories: those who do not expect to be caught, those who do not consider their acts to be "wrong," or those who are "out of control" and those whose acts are called "crimes of passion."

The goal of rehabilitation has failed for numerous reasons. The basic fallacy is that persons can be forcibly improved. From most prisoners' point of view, the "whole criminal justice system, with the penitentiary at the end of it, [is] an instrument of class and race oppression."[2] Practically, corrections systems have simply been unable to deliver rehabilitative services. "Nationwide, only 5 percent of the prison budget goes for services labeled 'rehabilitation' and in many states there is not even the pretense of making 'therapy' available to the adult offender."[3]

The very isolation of most prisons makes recruitment of counselors difficult; the elaborate security systems of both jails and prisons frustrate both volunteers and professionals who would deliver services. Finally, rapid turnover of prison population means that rehabilitative personnel do not even meet, much less get to know and work productively with prisoners.

Prisons are counterproductive of their intended purposes. To far too great an extent we continue to rely upon them out of a sort of inertia. Arguments in their favor are the prevailing ones and are, therefore, easier to defend than arguments which call for different responses to law violators.

Because during our lifetime prison is and has been synonymous with punishment, we assume too easily that prisons are traditional and necessary. However, only since the early nineteenth century have prisons become the conventional form of punishment in Europe and North America. Quakers were among the first to advocate

[1]William Nagel, *The New Red Barn: A Critical Look at the Modern American Prison* (New York: Walker & Co., 1973), p.139.

[2]Jessica Mitford, *Kind and Usual Punishment* (New York: Alfred A. Knopf, Inc., 1974), p. 232.
[3]*Ibid.*, p. 97.

the penitentiary model as a humane alternative to public shaming and corporal punishment. Eastern Penitentiary, established near Philadelphia in 1829, isolated prisoners from each other. The Quakers wanted prison to be a place where offenders could meditate on the Bible, repent, and return to society having "seen the error of their ways."

In the best case, we continue to rely on prisons because we fail to question prevailing assumptions. In the worst case, we use them to warehouse alcoholics, the mentally ill, and others with whom society is either unwilling or unable to cope in more constructive ways; or to warehouse many of the unemployed or unemployable; or to stifle dissent.

It is time to face the failure of prisons and to see them as Louk Hulsman, professor at Erasmus University, suggests: "a more important social problem than many of the social problems we are using the penal system to

⁴Louk H. C. Hulsman, "The Penal System as a Social Problem," May 3, 1974, Racine, Wisconsin.

solve."⁴ *There can be little doubt that prison increases the very alienation which causes crime.*

This view of prisons is especially valid for the Christian who is committed to working toward justice through reconciliation of victim, offender, and community.

In a teaching about prayer in chapter 7 of Matthew, Jesus indicates that human beings can have confidence in a loving God. God would no more respond in a capricious or arbitrary way to our prayers than would a loving parent give a stone when "his son asks for a loaf" or give a serpent when "he asks for a fish."

Jesus' probing questions are the sort of questions that should be raised about prisons and which Session 5 is designed to stimulate: Would a caring community, when one of its members is severely alienated and in deep trouble, put a person in an alienating institution? Would a caring community invest its resources in bricks and bars for prisons rather than for social services? Would a caring community not protest prison as a futile and destructive response to crime and look boldly for more effective and reconciling solutions?

SESSION 6—What Would a Caring Community Do?

SCRIPTURE: Revelation 3:22;
Matthew 25:31-46

TIME: 45 minutes to 1 hour

OBJECTIVE

To enable participants to see that an inclusive, caring community, in which all members are equally valued and truly interdependent, is the most effective deterrent to crime.

LEADER PREPARATION

Materials Needed:

Newsprint, felt-tip pens, masking tape

Advance Preparation

1. Prepare Newsprint Chart 1 for posting at the beginning of the session.

SESSION AT A GLANCE	
Web-charting	15 minutes
What is a caring community?	15 minutes
What would a caring church do?	15 minutes
Sharing and summary	10 minutes

2. Prepare Newsprint Charts 2 and 3 ("Causes of Crime" and "What Reduces Crime").
3. Prepare sufficient copies of Newsprint Chart 4 ("A Caring Community Is . . . ") for each small group.
4. Duplicate copies of Handout 1.

SESSION OUTLINE

As the Session Begins

State that this session explores how a "caring" community would respond to crime. In order to design responses that will make for safer communities, we need to think about the causes of crime. Review the "Session at a Glance" agenda and schedule.

Web-Charting (15 minutes)

Post Newsprint Chart 2.

CAUSES OF CRIME

Give the following instructions: "This is a form of brainstorming which we call web-charting. Please call out as many 'causes' as you can think of." After three minutes, ask participants if they see any connections between the various causes they have listed. With a felt-tip pen of another color, make the connecting links suggested by participants. Point out that the connections form a web.[1]

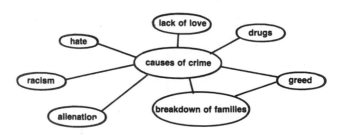

---

[1]Web-charting formats are adapted from *Mini Workshop Manual, Instead of Prisons*, PREAP, New York State Council of Churches, 1978.

Post Newsprint Chart 3.

```
┌─────────────────────────────────────────┐
│                                          │
│          WHAT REDUCES CRIME              │
│                                          │
│                                          │
│                                          │
│                                          │
└─────────────────────────────────────────┘
```

Say,"Now let's web-chart ways to reduce crime. Please call out as many ways as you can think of." After three minutes, ask participants to suggest the connecting links and again draw lines to form the web. Here is a typical set of responses.

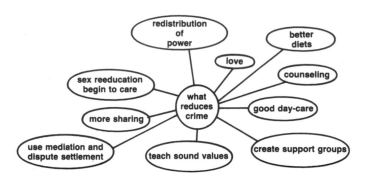

If there is any time remaining in the 15-minute period, ask participants to comment on any insights they have as they look at the two charts. You will have recorded *all responses* even if they seem inconsistent or even bizarre. It is possible, for example, that someone in your group will feel that lack of enough prisons, inadequate police vigilance, or some other insufficiency in the criminal justice system itself goes on the first chart. In such a case, you could point out that such answers are not really *causes* of crime, but are *responses* to it.

Leave the two web charts on the wall and *save* them for Session 7.

What Is a Caring Community? (15 minutes)

Ask participants to break into small groups of three to five persons. Give each group a copy of Newsprint Chart 4.

```
┌─────────────────────────────────────────┐
│                                          │
│        A CARING COMMUNITY IS . . .       │
│                                          │
│                                          │
│                                          │
│                                          │
│                                          │
└─────────────────────────────────────────┘
```

Ask each group to record as many responses as possible. After five minutes, ask participants to post their list. When all are posted, ask the participants to compare the list of key elements from their descriptions of a caring community with the second web chart. What conclusions can be drawn from this comparison?

What Would a Caring Church Do? (10 minutes)

In the same small groups, ask the participants to discuss how their church can model a caring community. What *one step* would they want their congregation to take toward being a more caring church?

Sharing and Session Summary (10 minutes)

After fifteen minutes, ask members of each small group to share their responses. Record them on newsprint (quickly) as they are reported.

Close the session with a reading of the litany based on Revelation 3:22.

Additional Scripture: Matthew 25:31-46.

LITANY ON A CARING CHURCH

LEADER: Those who have ears to hear, let them hear what the Spirit says to the churches. (See Revelation 3:22.)

RESPONSE: *LORD, HELP US TO HEAR.*

LEADER: Remind us that we are all your children. Help us to affirm one another's dignity.

RESPONSE: *LORD, HELP US TO CARE.*

LEADER: Make us mindful of those in need: the lonely, the labeled and outcast, the alienated, those in institutions.

RESPONSE: *LORD, HELP US TO KEEP YOUR COVENANT.*

LEADER: Each of us has some gift to share.

RESPONSE: *LORD, HELP US TO GIVE AND RECEIVE FREELY.*

LEADER: Make us mindful of those things which divide our community—greed, agism, racism, sexism, poverty, inequality.

RESPONSE: *LORD, HELP US TO MEND.*

LEADER: There are many divisions within our congregation—

RESPONSE: *LORD, HELP US TO REMEMBER THAT WE ARE THE CHURCH.*

LEADER: We live in a society where there is conflict and violence.

RESPONSE: *LORD, HELP US TO BE RECONCILERS, TO HEAL ALL WOUNDS, TO CONTINUE TO BUILD COMMUNITY.*

COMMUNITY: **Let us commit ourselves to making of this congregation a caring community, being alert to those situations in which reconciliation is needed. Let us hear what the Spirit says to the churches.**

SESSION 6—BACKGROUND READING

The Caring Community

The author of Acts was careful to point out that the earliest Christian community was a caring community. Twice in the first four chapters, he stated that every person in that community had all that was necessary (Acts 2:44-47; 4:32-35). The concerns of community members for each other were so great that people sold their possessions and brought the proceeds to the apostles to be distributed to the poor.

Greed and need interrupted the harmony of that little community. Ananias and Sapphira were greedy (Acts 5:1-11). They were willing to give much but not all of what they possessed to the community. The reason they reported that they were giving all was their need to be eligible for full support from the community. However, greed got the better of their generosity and they held back some of their money just in case the community should fail.

There were widows in that Greek community who were in need and who complained of hunger (Acts 6). The Hellenists (those of Greek nationality) believed "that their widows were neglected in the daily distribution" because the Hebrews had responsibility for the distribution.

The complaint of the Hellenist widows occasioned the commissioning of "the seven" to carry out the daily distribution but also signaled the breakdown of the caring community. The distribution duty was designated to "the seven" so that the religious leaders (the Twelve) could devote themselves "to prayer and to the ministry of the Word."

The minor injustices evidenced in this account were signals of the tensions that led to the later martyrdom of Stephen and to the great persecution which occurred as a result of Hebrew-Hellenist conflict in that first Christian community.

The Acts account points out that the caring community is a fragile system of relationships, laws, and institutions: a fragile system formed, molded, continually evaluated, and reformed by caring people. Such a community is not formed quickly, nor can it ever be taken for granted. If it is not faithful in its least task, it cannot be faithful in its greatest. Even though the Christian community meets to celebrate Word and sacrament, its relationships must always be measured by its concerns for the poorest and the weakest.

The very existence of the poor is evidence of injustice; the very existence of crime is evidence, also, that the caring community has broken down.

Is it unrealistic to measure our own efforts at building community against an ideal that even those zealous early Christians could not sustain? No, no more so than is any other way in which we test our efforts against what God expects of us. The failure to create a caring community is a spiritual failure. *If people do not move toward one another, they become more alienated and more likely to resort to crime.*

As was pointed out in earlier sessions, the disproportionate number of poor persons, often members of minority groups, who are caught up in the criminal justice system makes it clear that we must look at society itself for an explanation of crime.

Among professional criminal justice personnel, talk of crime reduction or crime prevention too often focuses not on societal causes but on more repressive measures, on more "ammunition" for the "war on crime." *These negative responses to lawbreakers surely perpetuate a vicious cycle of alienation—repression—increased alienation—more repression.*

In order to stop this vicious cycle, Christians should approach the problems of crime from a more fundamental and more humane perspective. We are committed to work toward a *just* society. *A caring community which met the needs of its members for self-esteem, for resources and services, and for a sense of community would be a more just society and one which experienced far less crime.*

Recognizing that no human community has ever achieved a state of completeness in terms of God's purpose, what do we—as Christians—believe "the spirit says to the churches" (Revelation 3:22)? What marks of a caring community can be suggested?

A caring community wants its laws to be no more restrictive than necessary to permit all persons to become all that they are capable of being.

A caring community watches over those unable to take care of themselves. No caring community would legislate, as have many states in the United States, that all juveniles charged with violent crimes would be tried in adult criminal courts. That sort of law directs the same antagonism society has had for the poor against its children. Surely, a caring community could protect itself against a few violently maladjusted children without pretending to hold them to adult responsibilities and standards of judgment. This solution would have us believe that society can only protect itself against such children by imprisoning them for long periods of time; in extreme situations for life.

A caring community never wants any of its members, young or old, to live or die in despair. It will use its resources to prevent crime rather than to build expensive prisons to lock away its failures.

A caring community wants to restore lawbreakers to an active role in society. The kind of response to crime we are describing is that of a proactive, not a defensive community. The caring community refuses to write off any person. No matter how estranged he or she may be from society through violent or destructive acts, the worth of this person is still recognized. The community will realize that to restore harmony among its members after a crime is seldom done easily or cheaply. Putting aside grievances is very difficult. This is especially so when the damage done by a crime is irreparable, as when there is loss of life or permanent mental or physical injury.

The mandate for Christians is to persevere. Jesus described the last judgment as being based upon the concern people showed for each other. But there was a special twist to Matthew's account (25:31-46). People who had fed the hungry, visited the sick or imprisoned, clothed the naked, and housed the homeless were told they had done this for Christ. In amazement, "the Just" turned to him and asked, "When did we see thee hungry and feed thee, or thirsty and give thee drink? And when did we see thee a stranger and welcome thee, or naked and clothe thee? And when did we see thee sick or in prison and visit thee?" Christ answered, "Truly, I say to you, as you did it to one of the least of these my brethren, you did it to me."

Notes on Scripture

Matthew 25:31-46 is a parable depicting the last judgment when nations will be separated as "a shepherd separates sheep from goats." Most scholars agree that The Gospel According to Matthew was written during the period between A.D. 80–100, soon after Jerusalem had been annihilated by the Romans in A.D. 70. Because Christians were being persecuted by the Romans and by Jews who feared that Christianity posed a threat of extinction to Judaism, members of the early church were beginning to waver.

Members of the church believed that even though Jesus was crucified and had been resurrected, it would be only a short period of time before he would return to set up his kingdom. Matthew used this parable in that historical context.

In verse 31 we read, "'When the Son of man comes in his glory, and all the angels with him, then he will sit on his glorious throne.'"[1] The concept of the "Son of man" who *will* come was Matthew's answer to those in his church with questions regarding the delay of Jesus' return. By depicting it as a future event, Matthew created time for building the church and preparing its members for the kingdom.

Matthew wanted to make the point that service to others was the essential qualification for finding favor with God:

Therefore, the true disciple shows mercy to others without calculation, without thinking that his deed will somehow cause God's judgment upon him to be more favorable. Such noncalculation grows out of a relation with Christ in which anxiety is diminished and the disciple responds to whatever human need is at hand, especially to his neighbor.[2]

The goal that Matthew set before early Christians is an invitation to be a caring community. If that goal is set before the contemporary church, it is an invitation to represent the caring community as we respond to the problem of crime.

[1]Herbert G. May and Bruce M. Metzger, eds., *The Oxford Annotated Bible* (New York: Oxford University Press, 1973), p. 1206.
[2]Robert A. Spivey and D. Moody Smith, Jr., *Anatomy of the New Testament* (New York: Macmillan, Inc., 1969), p. 127.

SESSION 7—Justice for Victims

SCRIPTURE: Luke 10:25-37

TIME: 45 minutes to 1 hour

OBJECTIVES

1. To look at those who are the victims of crime.

2. To view victims as persons who, like offenders, are in need of restoration to the community.

3. To explore the conditions within society which increase the likelihood of persons becoming victims of crime.

LEADER PREPARATION

Materials needed:

Newsprint, markers, masking tape
Web Charts from Session 6

Advance Preparation

1. Prepare Newsprint Chart 1.

```
SESSION AT A GLANCE
Victimization Awareness Quiz      15 minutes
Reporting                         10 minutes
Christian Response to Victims      10 minutes
Sharing                           10 minutes
```

2. Prepare Newsprint Charts 2 and 3 as shown in the Session Outline.

3. Duplicate copies of the Victimization Awareness Quiz, the answer sheet, and Christian responses to victims (Handouts 1, 2, and 3).

4. If possible, secure copies of *Grapevine*, November, 1977, "Loving Our Neighbors: Caring for Victims of Crime" (JSAC, 475 Riverside Drive, Room 1700A, New York, NY 10027).

5. Post the web charts from Session 6.

SESSION OUTLINE

Victimization Awareness Quiz (15 minutes)

Distribute copies of the quiz (Handout 1) to participants. After five minutes distribute the answer sheet (Handout 2) and ask participants to gather in small groups to discuss the quiz and the questions listed on Newsprint Chart 2.

```
Do you have new insights about victims?
Are offenders also victims?
Are those who work in criminal justice also
victims?
In a sense, are we all victims?
```

Reporting (10 minutes)

On Newsprint Chart 3 record at least one insight from each small group.

```
WHO ARE THE VICTIMS?
```

Refer to the web charts from Session 6. Ask participants to consider what would happen if the charts were entitled "Causes of Victimization" and "What Reduces Victimization." Ask if the same conditions in society which cause crime are those which cause victimization. Ask if the measures which reduce crime are the same as those which would reduce victimization.

Christian Responses to Victims (10 minutes)

Distribute Handout 3 to the small groups. Ask each group to select someone to read aloud Luke 10:25-37 and to lead discussion.

Sharing (10 minutes)

As summary for this session, ask participants to share their thoughts about "Justice for Victims" and about the responsibility placed on Christians by the concept of *tsedeqah*.

WHO ARE THE VICTIMS?

A Victimization Awareness Quiz

TRUE   FALSE

( )   ( )   1. Generally, we are much less likely to be victimized in our automobiles or homes than while walking the streets.

( )   ( )   2. Most victims of crimes of physical violence are white, middle class, and over thirty years of age.

( )   ( )   3. Banks and savings and loan institutions suffer their greatest losses through robbery.

( )   ( )   4. White-collar criminals, such as those who commit embezzlement, receive (when convicted) more severe sentences than robbers.

( )   ( )   5. Police spend the largest part of their time investigating serious crimes involving physical injury or property loss.

( )   ( )   6. Most "crimes against persons" involve blacks victimizing whites.

( )   ( )   7. In the past two centuries the homicide victimization rate has increased steadily.

( )   ( )   8. A majority of the largest corporations in the United States have victimized their customers and thereby, the public-at-large.

( )   ( )   9. Victims of crimes of physical violence or property loss often feel alienated from society and engage in antisocial behavior following their victimization.

( )   ( )   10. All fifty states have programs to compensate victims financially for their losses and medical expenses.

1. **FALSE** For example, in 1968 there were 53,000 traffic fatalities. "Studies in Michigan, California, and elsewhere have found that 65 percent of those responsible for fatal motor vehicle accidents had been drinking shortly before the impact and as many as 40 percent could be diagnosed as drunk." The same year, there were 13,650 homicides. Killings within families made up 31 percent of all murders in 1965; over half of those involved spouse killing spouse; 16 percent involved parents killing children.

The actual risk of victimization is relatively small. The rate for Index Crimes (those recorded by the FBI in the Crime Index—arson, rape, murder, robbery, aggravated assault, automobile theft, and larceny) remains constant at about 1.8 per 1,000 Americans.

(Quotation from Norval Morris, *The Honest Politician's Guide to Crime Control* [Chicago: University of Chicago Press, 1970], p. 62.)

2. **FALSE** The typical victim of crime, according to a Justice Department study published in 1976, is black, twelve to nineteen years old, and had an income of under $3,000.

(President's National Crime Commission Report "Challenge of Crime in a Free Society," Government Printing Office, 1967, p. 15, cited in L. Harold DeWolf, *Crime and Justice in America* [New York: Harper & Row, Publishers, Inc., 1975], p. 186.)

3. **FALSE** A 1974 FBI study revealed that such institutions lost more than 5½ times as much by embezzlement and fraud as by robbery.

(Harold DeWolf, *What Americans Should Do About Crime* [New York: Harper & Row, Publishers, Inc., 1976], p. 8.)

4. **FALSE** Most embezzlers, when caught, receive fines. For those who do receive prison terms, the average sentence is 15.3 months. The average sentence for robbers is 126.5 months.

(1974 Annual Report of the Director, Administrative Office of the U.S. Courts, Table D5, pp. A-54 and A-55, quoted in *Church and Society*, March-April, 1976, p. 48.)

5. **FALSE** "Half of the nation's police arrests and two-fifths of its $51 billion annual crime bill concern acts in which no person is hurt and no property is taken without the owner's consent . . . more than three million persons a year are laboriously processed . . . for such acts as public drunkenness, loitering, vagrancy, prostitution, gambling." These behaviors, often called "victimless crimes," are more vigorously prosecuted when public fear leads to cries for "law and order." During election years, as well, police sometimes find themselves under pressure to "clean up the streets."

(Edwin Kiester, Jr., *Crimes with No Victims*, Alliance for a Safer New York, 1972, pp.1, 4.)

6. **FALSE** An August 28, 1977, article in the *New York Times* stated, "In those cases where the ethnicity of both the victims and those arrested could be established 78.7% involved persons of the same racial backgrounds."

7. **FALSE** The homicide rate in the late 1960s was about 70 percent of the rate in the 1930s. Norval Morris indicates that the "rates of murder, non-negligent homicide, rape, and assault have all appreciably declined" since the 1870s. He concludes that the hysteria in the media about murder rates is not founded in historical fact.

(Norval Morris, *The Honest Politician's Guide to Crime Control* [Chicago: University of Chicago Press, 1970], p. 56.)

8. **TRUE** "In 1960, the Justice Department exposed a criminal conspiracy of the largest electrical manufacturers in the United States. Seven highly placed executives served short prison terms for their illegal activities which had cost the American people many millions of dollars. . . . about 60% of the largest corporations have been convicted in the courts of criminal business practices. . . ."

(L. Harold DeWolf, *What Americans Should Do About Crime* [New York: Harper & Row, Publishers, Inc., 1976], p. 8.)

9. **TRUE** A recent study, reported in the *New York Times,* August 28, 1977, has found that crime victims are often themselves arrested shortly following their own victimization.

10. **FALSE** In the decade of the 1970s less than half of the states had such programs. A victim must usually wait months for compensation. In New York in 1977 one-half of all claims were rejected; emergency awards were given to only 4 percent of the claimants.

("Loving Our Neighbors—Caring for Victims of Crime," *Grapevine*, publication of the Joint Strategy and Action Committee, Inc., vol. 9, no. 4 [November, 1977], p. 4.)

HOW SHOULD CHRISTIANS RESPOND TO VICTIMS?

And behold, a lawyer stood up to put him to the test, saying, "Teacher, what shall I do to inherit eternal life?" He said to him, "What is written in the law? How do you read?" And he answered, "You shall love the Lord your God with all your heart, and with all your soul, and with all your strength, and with all your mind; and your neighbor as yourself." And he said to him, "You have answered right; do this, and you will live."

But he, desiring to justify himself, said to Jesus, "And who is my neighbor?" Jesus replied, "A man was going down from Jerusalem to Jericho, and he fell among robbers, who stripped him and beat him, and departed, leaving him half dead. Now by chance a priest was going down that road; and when he saw him he passed by on the other side. So likewise a Levite, when he came to the place and saw him, passed by on the other side. But a Samaritan, as he journeyed, came to where he was; and when he saw him, he had compassion, and went to him and bound up his wounds, pouring on oil and wine; then he set him on his own beast and brought him to an inn, and took care of him. And the next day he took out two denarii and gave them to the innkeeper, saying, 'Take care of him; and whatever more you spend, I will repay you when I come back.' Which of these three, do you think, proved neighbor to the man who fell among the robbers?" He said, "The one who showed mercy on him." And Jesus said to him, "Go and do likewise" (Luke 10:25-37).

Discussion Questions

1. What did the Samaritan do to restore the victim of crime?

2. In our complex societies, who is the "neighbor" to the victim of crime?

3. Given the complexities of our society, in what ways would a Christian response be similar to that of the Samaritan? How would they differ?

4. How does the biblical concept of *tsedeqah* relate to this story?

SESSION 7—BACKGROUND READING

Justice for Victims

In Luke's Gospel we read a familiar story, the parable of the good Samaritan. This story was told in response to a lawyer who questioned Jesus about the steps he should take in order to inherit eternal life. When Jesus reminded him that the only requirements were to love God and to love your neighbor as yourself, the lawyer was not satisfied. He persisted with the question, "And who is my neighbor?"

As the story told by Jesus unfolds, we come to realize that all of the principals in it are neighbors, but that the priest and the Levite fail to act as neighbors to the man victimized by crime.

The man who fell among thieves on the road to Jericho is not described as good or bad. All the reader knows of him is his need. He is typical of the victim of crime: beaten, alone, and ignored by two-thirds of those who know his plight. The priest and the Levite are religious persons. The Samaritan is the despised foreigner traveling the road from Jerusalem to Jericho; yet it is he—at considerable risk to himself—who showed compassion for the victim.

When Jesus asked the lawyer, "Which of these three, do you think, proved neighbor to the man who fell among the robbers?", the answer was, "The one who showed mercy on him." And Jesus said to him, "Go and do likewise."

Session 7 asks participants to consider who is victimized and who ministers to the needs of victims in our complex society. A Law Enforcement Administration Agency (LEAA) survey in 1974 estimated that there were 24,600,000 direct victims of crime. These statistics included 20,600 homicides; 161,060 rapes; 383,040 personal robberies with injury; and 545,990 aggravated assaults with injury. The remaining offenses involved little physical contact or property loss: 5,641,160 larcenies under $50; 1,063,620 unsuccccessful larcenies and auto theft attempts; and 2,368,240 minor assaults.[1]

Despite the prevalence of victimization, few provisions are made in twentieth-century America for offering either compassion or compensation to our injured neighbors. *Victims are too often the forgotten persons when crime occurs.*

[1]Stephen W. Angel, Fay Honey Knopp, and Harold DeWolf, "Loving Our Neighbors: Caring for Victims of Crime," *Grapevine*, Joint Strategy and Action Committee, Inc., New York, vol. 9, no. 4 (November, 1977), p. 1.

Some victims have no one to counsel them about the trauma they experience when they have been injured or deprived of a valued possession—when their very person or home has been violated.

Some victims experience long delays and even harassment when they attempt to file claims or to serve as witnesses for the prosecution.

Some victims are more visible than others. Children beaten by their parents receive sympathy, care, and attention if their ordeal is publicized. However, should they become battering parents themselves, society may well forget their earlier ordeal and cry for vengeance.

Some victims are not thought of as victims because of their place in society. In his statement after the Attica prison uprising in 1971, Governor Rockefeller said, "Our hearts go out to the families of the hostages who died at Attica." He did not mention the families of the prisoners killed during the retaking of the prison by law enforcement personnel. One of those victims was Elliot James Barkley who went to prison originally for forging a money order for $124.60, at the age of eighteen. His only other criminal offense was driving without a license, a parole violation for which he was returned to Attica prison shortly before the uprising.[2]

If the pain, anger, and fear of victims are not dealt with, then victims become alienated—from their assailant and from all of the "neighbors" who failed them in their time of need.

Each one of us falls victim to certain crimes. It is estimated that 15 percent of the cost of any product or service is related to workplace crime. Tax bills are higher because of fraud and waste in government. Estimates are that Americans steal up to 5 percent of the gross national product, some $65 billion dollars, from themselves and then have to make restitution through higher insurance premiums, higher prices, and higher taxes.

Every crime takes a financial toll and has a negative effect on the quality of life. It is ironic that those least able to withstand the loss of income and/or added medical expenses are those most often victimized by physical violence and by property loss.

Like the offenders who are prosecuted for crime, the victims of crime in the United States are most often poor and nonwhite. They are twice as likely to be stabbed, and more than five times as likely to be shot; the victims

[2]Herman Badillo and Milton Haynes, *A Bill of No Rights* (New York: E. P. Dutton, 1972), pp. 132-133.

of pickpockets twice as often; and of robbery, aggravated assault, and motor vehicle theft more frequently. Black females are four times more likely to be raped than white females. Whites are more likely to be victims only of grand larceny.[3]

When this picture of the typical victim emerges, we are again reminded of the caring community's special responsibility to "the least of these." The Samaritan's response of unconditional love and of attention to every need serves as a model of how we should care for victims. Creative justice for victims requires "listening and loving" and helping them to be "forgiving." Rape crisis centers, victim-witness assistance programs, and shelters for battered women have been established by "Samaritans" who listened to the needs of victims. Community dispute centers are creative responses by "Samaritans" who want to resolve the basic conflict between persons who need to be reconciled to each other.

We are all travelers on the road from Jerusalem to Jericho and are confronted, almost every day, by some challenge to concretize our love for our neighbor who is victimized by violence or by some form of exploitation. Justice for victims involves "making right"—*tsedeqah*—at the level of immediate need and at the level of attacking the cause of crime.

Notes on Scripture

The parables found in the Bible represent a unique kind of story. Unlike myths and legends, which reinforce the world view of a people, parables *confront* moral understandings and standards of people in order to open up their minds to new realms of possibility and truth.

In the New Testament, the parables of Jesus are usually linked with his proclamations about the kingdom. Life in the kingdom, as Jesus presents it, will be radically different from anything we have come to accept as "normal." No wonder the Pharisees, who stood for the status quo, were disturbed by what Jesus said. By the standards of their society, they were, in a sense, "first"; but Jesus taught that the "first shall be last" (see Matthew 20:1-16)!

Jesus' use of the parables gives us some indication of his unusual skill as a teacher. These stories do not allow the hearer to remain aloof, but rather involve and surprise him or her. Jesus used the everyday images of his society, so that his audience would have no difficulty following the story line. But just when they would expect the story to end one way, Jesus would add an unexpected twist. His parables were often upsetting; in fact, they were intended to throw people off base!

The story of the good Samaritan is an excellent example of a parable with a surprise. Jesus' hearers were familiar with the "triadic" story form. (See Matthew 25:14-30; Luke 14:18-20; and 20:10-12.) According to this popular type of story, the audience would expect, after hearing about the priest and the Levite, that the third character would be an Israelite lay person. Hence, the parable would have an anti-clerical message. Imagine how shocked they must have been to learn that the third character—the one who fulfilled the duty of love—was a Samaritan. In this way Jesus drives home the point that our "neighbor" is not simply another member of our own tribe or clan. The example of the despised Samaritan was intended to teach the questioner that no human being is beyond the range of our love and kindness.[4]

Joseph P. Russell sums up the function of the parables when he says:

Parabolic religion, which Jesus represented, forces us out of our safe systems of accepted knowledge and understanding and confronts us with uncertainty and confusion so that we can move into deeper realms of reality. . . . We do not tell parables to answer questions or to resolve issues; we tell them with the deliberate intention of *raising* questions and of forcing the hearers to re-examine their assumptions about life and death.[5]

[3]Drawn from research of Terence Thornberry and Robert Figlio, cited in L. Harold DeWolf, *Crime and Justice in America* (New York: Harper & Row, Publishers, Inc., 1975), pp. 185ff.

[4]Joachim Jeremias, *The Parables of Jesus* (New York: Charles Scribner's Sons, 1963), pp. 204-205.

[5]Joseph P. Russell, *Sharing Our Biblical Story* (Minneapolis: Winston Press, Inc., 1979), p.14.

SESSION 8—Designing New Responses

SCRIPTURE: 2 Corinthians 5:18-19

TIME: 45 minutes to 1 hour

OBJECTIVES

1. To encourage participants to begin to look beyond the current mind-set which too often assumes that punishment is a solution when conflict occurs.

2. To explore more conciliatory, problem-solving approaches to conflict which take into account the context of the situation and the needs of the individuals involved.

LEADER PREPARATION

Materials needed:

Newsprint, markers, masking tape
Paper and pencils

Advance Preparation

1. Prepare Newsprint Chart 1.

```
SESSION AT A GLANCE
Society Building Exercise          15 minutes
New Designs for Problem Solving    15 minutes
Reporting and Discussion           15 minutes
```

2. Duplicate Handouts 1, 2, and 3. Cut Handout 1 into three sections.

3. Prepare Newsprint Chart 2 for the Reporting Section.

SESSION OUTLINE

Society Building Exercise (15 minutes)

Ask the participants to form groups of three to five persons and to choose a recorder who will record the key elements of the group's decisions about each of the Situation/Tasks in the Society Building Exercise.

Distribute Situation/Task 1 and ask the groups to make their decision in 5 minutes. At the end of 5 minutes, distribute Situation/Task 2. At the end of another 5 minutes distribute Situation/Task 3.

Do not discuss their decisions at this point but ask them to continue with:

New Designs for Problem Solving (15 minutes)

Distribute Handout 2. Emphasize that each group will have only 15 minutes to create a New Design for Problem Solving. At the end of that time, the recorder will share each small group's decisions with the total group.

Reporting and Discussion (15 minutes)

Record each small group's decisions and designs on Newsprint Chart 2.

SYSTEM FOR SHARING WATER	SANCTION TO BE APPLIED	WAS SANCTION TO BE APPLIED EQUALLY?	NEW DESIGNS FOR PROBLEM SOLVING

After each group has reported, try to elicit from the participants their insights about problem solving, about how their designs relate to the concept of *tsedeqah*, and about any conscious differences between their designs and the current criminal court process.

Give participants Handout 3 at the close of the session.

SOCIETY BUILDING EXERCISE

(to be cut into three sections)

SITUATION 1: Following a nuclear holocaust, there are nine survivors in an area. As far as they can ascertain, no one else remains on earth. The nine persons are:

1. John, a physician
2. Bob, a teacher
3. Sara, an engineer
4. Larry, a clergyman
5. Jim, who has not contributed to the group's needs (for example, he wouldn't help build the shelter; he refuses to participate in group meetings)
6. Yourself
7. Sue, a nursing mother
8. Bill, an architect and Sue's husband
9. Their infant daughter

SITUATION 2: It is discovered that the water supply is diminishing more rapidly than it would if everyone were taking only his or her share. A meeting is called to consider the situation.

SITUATION 3: Sue (the mother) and John (the physician) confess to taking more water than they are entitled to. Jim (the noncontributor) is *caught* taking more than his share.

TASK 1: The food supply seems to be plentiful (wild berries, etc.), but the water supply is limited. Establish a system for sharing the water that will make it last as long as possible.

TASK 2: Decide what action (sanction) should be taken if it is discovered that a member of the community is responsible for the disappearance of the water.

TASK 3: Discuss the consequences of applying to these three people the sanction decided upon in Task 2.

NEW DESIGNS FOR PROBLEM SOLVING

In the Society Building Exercise, the needs of the three persons who took more than their share of water were very different from one another. In our society, if the ''guilt'' or ''innocence'' of these three persons were determined through adversarial process in a trial or by plea bargaining, the judge would hear only the ''facts'' selected by the defense and prosecuting attorneys. Technically, if all are found guilty, all would be subject to the identical sanction.

In your small group, however, you are free to design a new process for assessing the behavior of the persons taking more than their share of water. You have a unique opportunity to create a process which will foster the inclusion of the offenders into the community and which will restore the community's torn fabric.

Before deciding upon a process, imagine yourself in the positions of each of the following:

SUE: Even though the community believed that its system of sharing water was fair, you felt that you needed more water than you were allowed. Your baby is your only child and you would do almost anything to maintain its health.
In an adversary court situation, your beliefs and feelings would be virtually irrelevant.

JOHN: Before the nuclear holocaust, you had been accustomed to never being without anything which you needed or wanted. You had never experienced hunger or thirst. However, since the community designed its system for sharing the water supply, you have been thirsty continuously. It had gotten to the point that you felt that you could no longer tolerate the discomfort.
In an adversary court situation, your feeling would be virtually irrelevant.

JIM: As a child, you were frequently abused. You learned very early in life that if you wanted or needed something, you had to take it. No one has ever cared much for you; so you never learned to care for others.
In an adversary court situation, this information would be irrelevant.

THE COMMUNITY: When you devised your system of sharing water, you were convinced that it was the most equitable one possible under the circumstances. The actions of these three persons have threatened the smooth functioning and perhaps even the survival of the community.

Your task is to create a design which:

- takes into account the needs of the offenders;
- takes into account the needs of all victims; takes into account the needs of the community;
- is educative (that is, contributes to the growth of all persons and to the strengthening of the community).

What is your approach?

THE NEED FOR NEW MODELS

Quotations for Reflection

Gilbert Cantor, an attorney from Pennsylvania, calls for the replacement of punishment with a new model of "restitution and responsibility."

He says, "The goal is the *civilization* of our treatment of offenders . . . (that is) to bring offenders under the civil, rather than the criminal law . . . and to move in this area of endeavor from barbarism toward greater enlightenment and humanity."

"An End to Crime and Punishment," *The Shingle,* Journal of the Philadelphia Bar Association, May, 1976.

". . . conflicts often signal a more pervasive problem between the parties than is reflected in the charges submitted to the court, but judges are permitted to see only the symptoms—the surface evidence—of it. Much like the visible tip of an iceberg, the private criminal complaint frequently deals with relatively minor charges growing out of deeper human conflict, frustration, and alienation; the criminal law with its focus on the defendant is ill-equipped to deal with this basic fact. . . . This is not problem-solving. . . . At best, a shaky truce may have been ordered."

Josh Stulberg, "A Civil Alternative to Criminal Prosecution," 39 *Albany Law Review* 359, 360-61 (1975).

U.S. Court of Appeals Chief Judge, David Bazelon, contends:

"The public needs to be educated about the nature of crime itself. In my opinion, there is only one genuine way to understand crime, and causation is its name.

"As a federal judge for the last 30 years, I have seen the human and social wreckage of our society. I've seen it flow through my courtroom in an undiminished stream. I can't avoid facing the relationship between crime and our unjust social structure."

"Alternatives for a Safer Society: New Responses to Crimes and Victims," slide show prepared by PREAP for Safer Society Press, New York, 1979.

In his court, they sentence themselves

BY ARNOLD DIBBLE
United Press International
Reprinted by permission of United Press International.

WINONA, Minn.—In the Winona County court of Dennis A. Challeen, who looks more like a heavy in a western movie than a judge, more than 30 adults guilty of misdemeanors sentence themselves every month.

Since late 1972, more than 3,000 miscreants have worked out their own sentences under the Winona County Court Self-Sentencing Program. The results have been unusual, productive and sometimes startling.

The program is believed to be the first of its kind. Occasionally judges have sentenced the guilty, particularly juveniles, to work penalties, but the Winona program is a sustained one for grown men and women.

Self sentences already on record range from a man who agreed to make restitution by replacing stained glass in a county building to a young thief who agreed to go to work for a mobile home dealer he ripped off. Today he is a partner in the firm.

Others:

● A young college youth guilty of reckless driving who agreed to work off his $100 fine by volunteering to help "The Save Lake Winona Project."

Result: He organized a rummage sale auction and raised more than $500.

● A 20-year-old who stole lumber from a farmer. He worked off a 30-day jail sentence by painting a building for the farmer.

Result: The farmer liked the job so well he hired the youth to paint three other buildings. They are now the best of friends.

● A 30-year-old man guilty of stealing eight automobile aerials. He agreed to work off a 30-day jail sentence by locating the owners of the cars and making restitution. He put an ad in the paper and had 45 claimants. "It just shows you how many dishonest people there are," Challeen said.

● A 65-year-old chronic shoplifter who agreed to put up $50 with the court. A miserly type, he was told he could lift anything and the court would pay.

Result: The miser quit shoplifting because he wanted his $50 back.

The program is entirely voluntary and has worked so well that there is only a 2 per cent repeat rate compared with up to 50 per cent recidivism in large cities.

Those found guilty usually are referred to James Heinlen, senior services officer of the court, who has been counseling juveniles and adults for more than 20 years. Between them they work out a plan utilizing what the misdemeanant can do best, and it is then presented to Challeen, who can accept or reject.

"I got the idea when I was a defense attorney," Challeen said. "I found out that the guilty defendant had a much better idea of what should be done than anyone else, but his feelings were just ignored."

Challeen, 40, was born in Braham, Minn., south of Duluth. He attended Stout University in Menomonie, Wis., on an athletic scholarship, the University of Minnesota, majoring in mechanical engineering, and worked his way through the William Mitchell College of Law in St. Paul.

He is a giant of a man who sits in his quarters in a blacksmith's sleeveless leather vest and open shirt. His Pancho Villa mustache rises and falls with his intense enthusiasms.

He calls himself a river rat and insists that after law school he just drifted down the Mississippi to Winona and now lives on a houseboat tied up to the island. He likes to live, and he's big on houseboat parties.

The self-sentence case he likes the best is the alcoholic who bet a 14-day jail sentence he could quit for six months. He fell off the wagon after five and voluntarily turned himself into the jail to serve his term. After he got out he committed himself to treatment at the state hospital.

"You know," the judge said. "Today, two years later, he has completely recovered and is working with alcoholics."

SESSION 8—BACKGROUND READING

Designing New Responses

Our society, the church included, is largely without visions, which means without clear and adequate goals. The result is rootlessness and instability. And that is what our life on our little island has become. God did not create us to be island dwellers. God created us to be the vanguard of the kingdom. We need to rebuild our ship and set sail with Christ. However, we will never be inspired or enabled to do that without a vision. . . .

That vision [of God's kingdom] is not unreal. It is a motivating force, a hope by which to live, and a direction in which to travel. Throughout Scripture the people of God, when they are most faithful, live by God's vision for them and for the world. But "where there is no vision, the people perish" (Prov. 29:18, KJV).[1]

"God did not create us to be island dwellers," said Christian educator John Westerhoff. True enough. But Session 8 is based on the assumption that it is sometimes useful or necessary to imagine ourselves on a deserted island in order to get enough perspective on ourselves and our social arrangements to be able to engage in evaluation and redesign.

We cannot be "the vanguard of the kingdom" unless we understand our nature, our relationship to God, and unless we carefully examine the social arrangements we have made and wish to make, and the role of the church in fulfilling these arrangements.

Consciously or unconsciously, each of us has a view of human nature, and that view affects how we respond to other persons, as well as the motives and attributes which we ascribe to them. Furthermore, the view of human nature which we collectively adopt influences the character of our social institutions and how effectively they encourage responsible behavior.

> . . . if we are convinced that we are innately evil, we will design the institutions of our culture according to that definition. Psychological definitions of the human state can thus become self-fulfilling prophecies. We may not be what we think we are, but what we think we are will determine in great part what we are to become. We must not design our

[1]John H. Westerhoff, *Tomorrow's Church, A Community of Change* (Waco, Texas: Word Books, 1976), p. 37.

future in terms of our current disillusionment, for those designs, even if erroneously conceived, will influence the future development of our species.[2]

Ironically, Christianity as it has emerged in the United States has often contributed to a negative view of humankind, a view which overemphasizes the human capacity for sinfulness and evil. However, a closer look at our biblical tradition challenges us to develop a more positive outlook, for it teaches us that we are *all* children of God.

It is in the criminal justice system that our negative views on human nature are all too clearly revealed, as if under a magnifying glass. Persons are seen as evil if not controlled, as irresponsible, unchangeable, and innately hostile toward law and the structures of society. It is assumed that offenders lack the ability to develop their own internal controls and that it is necessary to apply external controls in order to limit unacceptable behavior. It is assumed, also, that offenders cannot be motivated to make restitution to their victims.

Thus, individual growth is thwarted, and victims and community are shortchanged. Persons are acted upon instead of being encouraged to become responsible actors in negotiating their own resolutions to the conflict which occurred. Biblical views would require an offender to confront his or her own wrongdoing, seek to make amends, and to embark on a new course.

In present court procedures, responsibility is thwarted. Situations are addressed without their own context. When the prosecutor and the defense attorney are pitted against each other as adversaries, truth is often subverted by legal technicalities and "winning" takes precedence over resolving the original conflict. In cases which are prosecuted, punishment is often so severe that the offender and his or her family feel victimized by the state and become more alienated.

Community is thwarted, also. The original fracture of relationships is not healed but is left to fester. Too fre-

[2] Willard Gaylin, "Caring Makes the Difference," *Psychology Today,* August, 1976, p. 39.

quently the agents of society do not offer models of reconciliation, but they themselves perpetuate the dynamics of manipulation and even, in some cases, of violence.

When we redesign and "rebuild our ship," we will have to *give attention to the positive ways in which people can be motivated to comply with community standards*. As members of the community of faith who have responsibility for preventing and resolving conflict, we will need to model the behavior that we hope to induce.

While it is true that individuals learn from widely varying stimuli—negative as well as positive—for Christians there must be serious question about the value of negatively induced learning (punishment). Deliberate infliction of pain or psychic deprivation is counter to the reconciling and redeeming model of Christ. While outward compliance and control may be attained by punishment, the negatives which are internalized will inevitably manifest themselves in future behavior.

In Paul's letter to the Corinthians, he says that "if anyone is in Christ"—if anyone claims to be a Christian—he or she has been given *the ministry of reconciliation* (see 2 Corinthians 5:17-18). *Tsedeqah* is "making right": nurturing, healing, reconciling, building peace. The vision of God's kingdom is our hope and our motivating force for redesigning our communities, so that reconciliation may become a reality.

SESSION 9—Does the End Justify the Means?

SCRIPTURE: Proverbs 6:17-19

TIME: 45 minutes to 1 hour

OBJECTIVES

1. To engage participants in examining the nature of and the relationship between the ends and the means sometimes used in the criminal justice system.

2. To consider the legality, morality, and the social consequences of these means and ends.

LEADER PREPARATION

Materials needed:

Props (such as a wallet and bills, room dividers)

Advance Preparation

1. Prepare Newsprint Chart 1, "Session at a Glance."

```
SESSION AT A GLANCE
Role Plays
   Decoy                          10 minutes
   Immunity                       10 minutes
Debriefing and Discussion         25 minutes
Session Summary                    5 minutes
```

2. Duplicate Handouts 1, 2, and 3. Cut Handout 1 and Handout 2 into role cards for each of the characters in the "decoy" and "immunity" role plays.

3. Familiarize yourself with the instructions for role play.

4. Prepare the room arrangement by having the observers' chairs placed away from the center of the room but be certain that everyone can see the entire dramas. If feasible, use props (chairs, screens) to mark off distinct areas, such as inside and outside a building. Use the time before the second role play while players are assimilating their roles to set up for the second scene.

5. Write the "Questions for Discussion" on newsprint for posting.

SESSION OUTLINE

As the Session Begins

Review the "Session at a Glance" agenda and schedule. Explain that this session will use role play to raise questions about ends and means. Role plays are mini-dramas which allow persons to experience some of the feelings and thoughts of persons who are involved in situations in real life similar to the one enacted in the role play. The purpose of a role play is to provide both the players and observers with the kinds of insights into such situations that only direct experience normally permits and, at the same time, to engender greater empathy for those involved in the situation in real life.

Decoy Role Play (10 minutes)

Describe the scene of the first role play. Explain that each of the role plays portrays a common occurrence in the criminal justice system. The issues raised in each case revolve around the age-old question of means and ends.

The scene is at the local welfare office at four o'clock in the afternoon. John Smith is applying for public assistance. He will meet with Sally Jones, an eligibility worker at the Welfare Department. John's wife, Mary, will meet with John briefly while he's waiting to be seen by Sally. Outside the building, Bill Brown is lying on the pavement. He appears to be drunk.

Distribute the role cards. Do not share the information on them. To help the players get into their roles, ask that they think of other aspects of their role lives (family, jobs, friends, motivations, etc.) as well as those described on their cards.

Designate the rest of the participants as observers and tell them that their role is just as important as that of the players.

Give some signal for the role play to begin. Stop the actions after ten minutes (or earlier if the scene is obviously played out).

When Bill Brown arrests John Smith, stop the role

play. Thank the players and the observers and go directly into the role play on immunity.

Immunity Role Play (10 minutes)

Describe the scene as being in police headquarters. Jack and Tony are each being interrogated by investigating officers in separate rooms. So far, each has maintained his innocence about involvement with stolen property.

Distribute the role cards. While players are familiarizing themselves with their roles, arrange the props to indicate separate interrogation rooms.

Give some signal for the role play to begin. Stop the actions after ten minutes (or earlier if the scene is obviously played out). Jack should have been offered immunity in exchange for information. It should be obvious that Tony will not be offered immunity. Thank the players and observers.

Debriefing and Discussion (20 minutes)

Explain that debriefing is a very important part of a role play. People often become very involved in the roles which they play and experience feelings which surprise them. They also often have new insights about the experiences of persons who confront, in real life, situations similar to the ones acted out.

After all of the players are seated, ask each one to express how he or she felt to be in his or her role in the decoy and in the immunity dramas. Allow about five minutes for this.

Next, ask for observations about each role play from the rest of the participants. Make certain that observers understood the significance of the scenes and exactly what was happening. Allow about five minutes for this.

Engage in general discussion about the practices of the criminal justice system which have been portrayed. Ask the participants to consider and comment upon the following questions which you can post on newsprint:

Questions for Discussion

1. What questions of morality are involved in the use of decoys and immunity?

2. What are the attitudes of the "caught" about these means? Of the criminal justice personnel? Of the public?

3. Does the end always justify the means?

Session Summary (5 minutes)

As facilitator, you shouldn't try to "answer" these questions. The issues involved are very complex. Point out that you are trying to raise some important questions for further consideration.

Close with a thought from William Penn, written in 1693:

"A good end cannot sanctify evil means
Nor must we ever do evil that good may come of it.
Let us then try what love will do
For if men did once see we love them,
We should soon find they would not harm us.
Force may subdue. But love gains,
And he that forgives first, wins the laurel."

For an Extended Session

Discuss the Scripture: Proverbs 6:17-19.

"DECOY" ROLE CARDS

JOHN SMITH: You are thirty-five years old and have a wife, Mary, and four children. You dropped out of high school and have worked at odd jobs for years. Your last job was in a factory, but you were laid off a year ago. Your unemployment benefits have just run out and you haven't found other work. You are about to meet the eligibility worker at the welfare department. It is now 4:00 P.M. and you've been waiting since 5:30 this morning. When you have finished your interview with the eligibility worker, go outside the building where you will find a drunk with a $20 bill sticking out of his wallet.

MARY SMITH: John's wife. You are thirty years old and have four children. You love John, but tensions have been high since John lost his job a year ago. It has been especially bad the past two weeks. Frankly, you've had it. You have found someone to watch the kids for an hour and have gone to the welfare department to talk to John. You'll tell him that if he doesn't get some money to get the landlord off your back and to buy some groceries, that's it. Leave the office when the eligibility worker calls John.

SALLY JONES: You are an eligibility worker for the welfare department. It is now four o'clock and you have seen a steady stream of persons applying for assistance today. Many times you must send people away because they haven't filled out the forms properly. Your next client is John Smith. Shuffle your stack of eligibility forms while John and his wife, Mary, have a brief conversation. Then call John to your desk. He has not filled out the forms properly; so you will tell him to come back tomorrow.

Furthermore, you will inform him that, even if he is eligible, it will probably be a month before he can begin to receive assistance, since the department is overburdened. Do not spend much time with him because there is still a long line of persons to see before 5:00 P.M.

BILL BROWN: You are a police officer who has been assigned to work as a decoy. There have been muggings and purse-snatchings in your precinct, which is in the neighborhood of the welfare department. In order to catch some of these offenders, you are pretending to be a drunk who has passed out in front of the welfare building. Your wallet, with a few bills prominently displayed, is next to you. If John Smith takes your wallet, you are immediately to stand up and arrest him.

"IMMUNITY" ROLE CARDS

JACK: You're twenty-two years old and have been charged with fencing stolen property. You're known to have "questionable" associates and activities but have never been arrested before. Your friend, Tony, whom you met when he came to town four months ago was arrested, also, and is being questioned in another room.

FIRST INVESTIGATING OFFICER: You know that there's a lot of trafficking in stolen property. For a long time you've been trying to catch the persons who are responsible for the fencing. It's an election year and the police chief has been after you to make a move. Furthermore, the public is putting pressure on the department to stem the crime problem.

You will interrogate suspect Jack, charged with fencing stolen property. The suspect is known to have "questionable" associates, one of whom is Tony. Tony is being questioned by another officer about possession of stolen property. You and the other officer have agreed that you will offer immunity to Jack if he will tell you all he knows about the stolen property ring.

SECOND INVESTIGATING OFFICER: You know that there is a lot of trafficking in stolen property. For a long time you and the other officers have been trying to catch the persons who are responsible for the fencing. It's an election year, and the police chief has been after you to make an arrest. Furthermore, the public is putting pressure on the department to stem the crime problem.

You will interrogate suspect Tony, charged with possession of stolen property. Tony's friend, Jack, is being questioned by another officer about the sale of stolen property. You and the other officer have agreed that Jack will be offered immunity if he tells all he knows about the stolen property ring. Do not offer immunity to Tony because he doesn't appear to have much information.

TONY: You are twenty years old and have been charged with possession of stolen property (a radio given you by your friend Jack). You have lived in the city only four months and met Jack when you came to town. Jack was arrested, also, and is being questioned by investigating officers in another room.

Quotation for Reflection

USE OF POLICE DECOYS QUESTIONED

I APPRECIATED your full discussion of the police decoy issue (D&C editorial, Dec. 27). Though we obviously gave differing views and opinions, your presentation left very few stones unturned in representing both sides of this difficult question.

I expect that others will now enter the discussion and I would consider it salutary to hear from the Public Defender and District Attorney as well as Police Chief Hastings.

There are a few points I would have you consider before continuing to endorse decoys.

You describe the use of decoys as an example of police "enterprise." In my opinion, decoys are the lazy man's way to law enforcement.

On the issue of downtown economic viability, I wonder what effect the constant reports of those apprehended through the use of decoys has on those who may by considering doing business in the inner city? It would seem to me that this would only further discourage such endeavors. I doubt if it makes people "free of fear in the city"

I BELIEVE the real issue is our old nemisis, racism. Your editorial does not mention racism nor that the bulk of those apprehended through the use of decoys are minority persons.

No one is addressing the question of race and criminal justice, though the statistics are staggering. (The New York State prison population is now 74.5 percent minority and the federal prison population has risen by 12.1 percent in minorities in just 8 years.)

Inner city crime is merely the symptom. Racism—and the problems it engenders, such as unemployment—is the disease.

Finally, you mention that "criminal intent was already there in most instances." There are a lot of people walking around looking for criminal opportunities. The question is, should the police make these opportunities available in order to get these intent-bearing people off the street?

WE ALL have criminal intent at some time in our life. My feeling is that the more desperate we are, the more likely this intent will be expressed.

Is it our policy in this society to aggravate the desperation of the disadvantaged by luring them into crime and saddling them with felony convictions? Given the other failures of our criminal justice system, especially corrections, we may well be merely grooming another class of graduate criminal specialists once they have passed the decoy admissions test.

Again, thank you for bringing this issue to the public's attention. I look forward to additional comment on decoys in the weeks ahead.

JOHN IVES, Community Coordinator, Judicial Process Commission.

From *Democrat and Chronicle*, Rochester, New York, January 5, 1978.

SESSION 9—BACKGROUND READING

Does the End Justify the Means?

Most of us have a well-developed sense of injustice. It seems to be innate. We can remember, even when we were very young, the feelings of indignation that arose within us when our basic sense of fairness was violated. Perhaps we thought that a sibling received a larger piece of cake or that he or she was loved more than we. Probably we all remember when a teacher restricted all of the class because one member was acting out. Probably we remember, also, when we were the perpetrators of injustice—when we "got away" with some mischief for which we let someone else take "the blame."

If our sense of fairness is so acute in our personal lives, it should be helpful to explore whether we have that same sense of fairness in our community lives.

There are certain procedures used by the criminal justice system which must be included in our examination of how efforts to do justice go awry. The morality of using decoys to catch "criminals," the prevalence of plea bargaining, and offers of immunity from prosecution are three such areas open to question.

Let us look first at the use of decoys. Is it ever justifiable to set up the situation of a potential crime and sit back waiting for the bait to be taken? The rationale for using decoys is that it is only the "criminal type," the "habitual thief" who has been preying on neighborhood derelicts, who would bend down to take the enticing roll of bills sticking out of the "derelict's" pocket, who would be unable to resist this clear and unusual temptation. Can we rule out the possibility that a hungry person would respond to the bait? Or can we even justify the procedure if a habitual thief is caught? Have we thought about why that person became a "thief" in the first place?

Let us take another example, of a man driving through the downtown of a city late at night. Unaware that police are "cracking down" on prostitution, he is unprepared for the woman who approaches his car at a traffic light. His response is barely uttered before she identifies herself as a policewoman and arrests him for propositioning her. The real question is not whether he was saying "yes" or "no" but whether it is defensible to entice a passerby into such a situation from which he may emerge with a wounded reputation if not with a criminal conviction.

The most familiar shortcut in law enforcement is plea bargaining. As an inducement to a defendant to plead guilty, a prosecutor will offer to drop or reduce some charges or to recommend to the court a favorable sentence, or not to seek the maximum penalty. The origin of and the rationale for plea bargaining is efficiency. It is maintained by many court officials that plea bargaining is a necessity without which our courts would be overwhelmed by the vast number of cases to be tried.

The "end" of efficiency has many problematic side effects. First of all, the court takes on an atmosphere of bargain-basement justice. The kind of deal a defendant gets will be determined largely by such considerations as "the state of the court calendar, the resources available to the prosecutor or the court, the strength of the case against the defendant, the personal or political ambition of the prosecutor, and the relationship between the defense counsel and the judge or prosecutor." [1]

When the full resources of the court are brought against a defendant with few resources, there is tremendous pressure to "cop a plea." The defendant who is willing to admit responsibility (guilt) finds himself or herself involved in a game of charge bargaining, which is a distorted approach to leniency. The defendant who maintains a plea of innocence and decides on a trial faces the probability of a heavier sentence if found guilty of the original charges. [2] An additional element of jeopardy is at work in this situation because of the fact that police officers and prosecutors tend to "overcharge" as a response to the prevalence of plea bargaining.

What have we as a community taught the offender when we subject her or him to plea bargaining? Have we fostered forthrightness and have we engendered trust? Have we engaged the offender in exploring ways to make amends? The answer is a resounding "no," and we all lose because the court has succumbed to expediency. The most fundamental disagreement with plea bargaining is that the offender has little or no participation in the process, except for final acceptance or rejection of the plea. The result is that "for the defendant, the relationship between the act which led to the charge and the punishment which results, has become blurred." [3]

Immunity from prosecution, like plea bargaining, is

[1] Peter L. Zimroth, *New York Times Magazine*, May 28, 1972.
[2] Documented by Lesley Oelsner, *New York Times Magazine*, September 27, 1972. Cited in Jessica Mitford, *Kind and Usual Punishment* (New York: Alfred A. Knopf, Inc., 1973), pp. 83-85.
[3] Task Force on Courts, Report No. II, Church Women United, Rochester, New York, 1973, p. 19.

an option the criminal justice system may offer defendants who are assumed but not proved to be guilty. The idea behind immunity is to let some "small fish" get away if, in return, one nets some "larger ones." Information that can be used in prosecution of others is accepted in exchange for freedom, in the form of reduced sentences, or for immediate release.

The practice of offering immunity authorizes treachery and introduces the possibility of crimes of cowardice—fabricating the testimony wanted by the interrogators. It certainly discourages the virtues of courage and integrity. It shortcuts thorough investigations and sometimes tempts law enforcement personnel to round up "petty law violators" for the sole purpose of gaining information about more serious crimes they need to solve.

Throughout this curriculum there has been emphasis on the need for positive responses to problems of criminal justice. This session raises serious questions about the positive nature of certain responses. Entrapment, it would seem, could be evaluated on the principle that it is basically wrong to lure persons toward criminal acts; immunity on the basis that it is wrong to implicate another person for the sake of avoiding self-consequences; and plea bargaining on several bases, the most important being that the process blurs the significance of the defendant's act. Any shortcut or procedure that stresses "making an arrest" or "getting a conviction" over the doing of justice is surely unacceptable.

In addition to the validity of our responses we need, once again, to evaluate our motives. The poor, black, and Hispanic are most pressured by plea bargaining, and entrapment is most frequently directed toward the "street criminal" and the "street walker" (not the call girl). Immunity is the only one of the three practices that is used extensively in the prosecution of "white collar" crimes.

If we are concerned about the moral dimensions of our responses to crime, the church must continue to search Scripture and tradition for perspectives on our dilemma. In 1973 the U.S. Catholic Conference raised a question about the entire notion of general deterrence:

> It is necessary in any case to raise serious moral objection to tormenting one man unjustly in order to instruct or caution another.[4]

Such questions challenge us all to rethink the "means" we use to achieve the "end" of a safer society.

[4]United States Catholic Conference, "The Reform of Correctional Institutions in the 1970s," Washington, D.C., 1973.

Many thoughtful commentators believe that the crisis in criminal justice is a crisis in our ethical values. Professor Harold Berman of Harvard Law School says that "Western man is undergoing an integrity crisis." People are experiencing "disillusionment with law and with religion. There are, of course, many causes. One of them, I believe, is the too radical separation of one from the other."[5] "At the highest level, surely, the just and the holy are one—or else not only all men but the whole universe, and God himself, are condemned to an eternal schizophrenia."[6] Berman contends that "people will desert institutions that do not seem to them to correspond to some transcendent reality in which they believe."[7]

Anne Strick is a writer and a congressional secretary who was exposed, over a five-year period and in various roles, to both civil and criminal court procedures. Our court procedures, she finds, have isolated the context and personal relationships of life. The adversary method perpetuates in our national life the moral schizophrenia which results from espousing cooperation and loving kindness but acting on competition and dominance. "As means and ends are inseparable," says Strick, any "new legal system must exemplify that ethic it claims to value."[8]

The debate on "means " and "ends" is as old as recorded history. The book of Genesis (chapter 3) indicates that, from the beginning, humankind was loath to take responsibility for actions. When God questioned Adam, he testified against Eve, who in turn implicated the serpent. God accepted the testimony of each but gave immunity to no one. Would our view of ethics be different, today, if God had granted Adam immunity for his testimony against Eve?

The Bible speaks to our condition precisely because it deals with the hard questions. It details moments of human greatness and of human weakness. It says that God is the constant moral force. God does not grant immunity for the consequences of our actions; God does not bargain; God does not entrap. The Bible indicates that God is to be trusted; one person is not set over against another.

A portion of the Wisdom Literature in Proverbs is a good test by which to evaluate the practices questioned in Session 9:

[5]Harold J. Berman, *The Interaction of Law and Religion* (Nashville: Abingdon Press, 1974), pp. 21, 23.
[6]*Ibid.*, pp. 137-138.
[7]*Ibid.*, p. 73.
[8]Anne Strick, *Injustice for All* (New York: G. P. Putnam's Sons, 1977), p. 208.

There are six things which the Lord hates,
seven which are an abomination to him:
haughty eyes, a lying tongue,
and hands that shed innocent blood,
a heart that devises wicked plans,
feet that make haste to run to evil,
a false witness who breathes out lies,
and a man who sows discord among brothers.
—Proverbs 6:16-19

Notes on Scripture: Wisdom Literature

The Book of Proverbs belongs to a larger literary genre found within the Bible known as the "Wisdom" literature. In Israelite society, the priest, the prophet, and the sage were the traditional teachers. To the priestly class belonged instruction regarding religious ritual; the prophets spoke on behalf of Yahweh to the nation; and the wise (sages) counseled about conduct pleasing to Yahweh in everyday situations. While elements of the Wisdom tradition can be found throughout the Old Testament, the books of Job, Ecclesiastes, and Proverbs are its major representatives in the canon.

Wisdom literature was common throughout the ancient Near Eastern world—in Egypt and Mesopotamia, for example—as well as in Israel. It has a cosmopolitan and universal character, which sharply distinguishes it from the more nationalistic character of the prophetic utterances. As in Egypt, Israelite wisdom originally flourished in the court, and thus often seems to be directed to those who move in "polite" society. Yet, in Israelite wisdom literature, more than elsewhere, Israel's wisdom exhibits a "leveling" tendency, perhaps due to the destruction of Jerusalem and the exile in Babylon.

In the Book of Proverbs, it is possible to discern the characteristics of the wise person. First of all, one who is wise is genuinely religious. The wise person knows and heeds God's commandments and knows that God is just in dealing with persons. He or she is likely to be fairly prosperous, since Yahweh regards the piety of the wise. Yet such a person would not be enormously wealthy, since extreme riches would likely have been acquired through exploitation of the poor and are a sign of an ungenerous spirit. The wise person is moderate in all things and shows prudence in conversation. He or she has sufficient leisure for reflection upon the meaning of life and the path of true wisdom. The wise person will not seek the company of idle people, will not gossip about his or her neighbors, and will never bear false witness before judges.

Tradition attributes the authorship of Proverbs to King Solomon (circa 1,000 B.C.). This tradition partly stems from the account in 1 Kings 3:16ff. of his judicial insight and of his utterance of fables and proverbs in 1 King 4:29ff. It may indeed be true that Solomon founded a wisdom school, and that he had sages within his court. However, our Book of Proverbs was probably written by many wise persons and compiled after the Exile (i.e., after 500 B.C.) as a "code of conduct" for Jews living in scattered communities during the Diaspora. The wise became the principal teachers in postexilic Judaism, where the voice of the prophet was no longer heard and the careful organization of the cult no longer possible.

The Hebrew word for proverb is *mashal*, which literally means "comparison." However, the root from which *mashal* is taken also means "to have authority" or "to rule." Hence, a proverb is an "authoritative word," intended to provide instruction regarding proper conduct. For the Jew, the motive for proper conduct—and the motive behind the compilation of the Book of Proverbs—is set forth in the very beginning of the book: "The fear of the LORD is the beginning of knowledge" (1:7).

For more information, see:

Forestall, J. Terrence, "Proverbs" in the *Jerome Biblical Commentary*, ed. Raymond E. Brown et al. Englewood Cliffs, N.J.: Prentice Hall, Inc., 1968. pp. 495-505.

Greenstone, Julius, *Proverbs: With Commentary*. Philadelphia: Jewish Publication Society of America, 1950.

Harrelson, Walter, *Interpreting the Old Testament*. New York: Holt, Rinehart and Winston, Inc., 1964.

Rylaarsdam, J. C., "Hebrew Wisdom," in *Peake's Commentary on the Bible*, ed. M. Black and H. H. Rowley. Nashville: Thomas Nelson, Inc., 1962. pp. 386-390; 444-457.

Sanders, James A., *Torah and Canon*. Philadelphia: Fortress Press, 1972.

SESSION 10—Thou Shalt Not Kill

SCRIPTURE: Exodus 21:24 and Matthew 5:38-42; Deuteronomy 30:15-20 and 1 Peter 2:13-14; Hosea 6:8 and Romans 13:1-6

TIME: 45 minutes to 1 hour

OBJECTIVES

1. To become aware that the way a society treats the most alienated of its members is a true index of its esteem for human life, which is God's image and gift.

2. To study those Old and New Testament passages which, misinterpreted, have reinforced retributive practices.

3. To become aware that, according to Scripture, only God may take life; humans are to cultivate, cherish, and develop it.

Note: Since the issues of the death penalty are of central concern to our Judeo-Christian heritage, and because state-sanctioned killings have resumed in the United States, we have included two sessions on this topic. Session 10 is designed to help participants examine their own attitudes toward this ultimate sanction. Session 11 continues this examination but has more emphasis on the application of the death penalty.

LEADER PREPARATION

Materials needed:

Newsprint, markers, masking tape
Bibles

Advance Preparation

1. Prepare Newsprint Charts 1, 2, and 3.
2. Make copies of Handouts 1, 2, 3, 4, and 5.

SESSION OUTLINE

Opinionnaire (3 minutes)

Distribute copies of the Opinionnaire on the Death Penalty. Allow three minutes for participants to complete them. Do not collect them and do not discuss them at this time.

SESSION AT A GLANCE	
Opinionnaire	3 minutes
Pros and Cons of the Death Penalty	5 minutes
Study and Reflection	20 minutes
Exodus 21:24 and Matthew 5:38-42	
Deuteronomy 30:15-20 and 1 Peter 2:13-14	
Hosea 6:8 and Romans 13:1-6	
Essays by Miller and Hammer	
Reporting and Discussion	15 minutes
Session Summary	2 minutes

Pros and Cons of the Death Penalty (5 minutes)

Engage participants in listing all the arguments favoring the death penalty and all the arguments opposing the death penalty. Record them on Newsprint Chart 2.

ARGUMENTS FOR THE DEATH PENALTY	ARGUMENTS AGAINST THE DEATH PENALTY

Do not discuss these arguments at this time. Save this newsprint for Session 11.

Study and Reflection (20 minutes)

Ask the participants to gather into three groups. Distribute Bibles and copies of the essays by Rabbi Miller and Dr. Hammer, Handouts 2 and 3. Ask each group to select a recorder and spokesperson.

Refer to the "Session at a Glance" chart. Assign one pair of Scripture passages to each of the three groups.

Note that for each pair one may seem to support the death penalty, while the other more obviously seems to oppose it. Suggest that careful study of the passages in light of their context in the entire Scripture would show that the Christian ethic stands opposed to state-sanctioned executions.

Note also the essays. Rabbi Miller points out that the law codes of the Old Testament must be viewed in their historical and cultural contexts. The Jewish Scriptures, in fact, placed a high value upon human life and underscored God's sovereignty. Even after the closing of the Jewish canon, there has been an ongoing interpretation of the Torah by Jewish Rabbis.

Professor Hammer points to the need to scrutinize biblical texts carefully, using the tools of biblical analysis (as in the Word Study in Session 2). Too often, Scripture has been "proof texted" to support ideologies and practices which are counter to the Christian faith.

Ask each group to discuss the implications of the death penalty, drawing on:
- the Scripture passages
- the essays
- previous work on the concept of *tsedeqah* justice.

Reporting and Discussion (15 minutes)

Record the key points of the insights of each of the three groups on Newsprint Chart 3.

```
┌─────────────────────────────────────────────┐
│                                             │
│   IMPLICATIONS OF THE DEATH PENALTY         │
│                                             │
│                                             │
│                                             │
│                                             │
└─────────────────────────────────────────────┘
```

Refer to the Pro and Con Arguments (Newsprint Chart 2). Ask whether the majority of insights fall in the "Pro" or the "Con" columns. Guide the discussion on the assumptions in the Background Readings for Session 10 and Session 11.

Session Summary (2 minutes)

Ask participants to reflect on their responses to the Opinionnaire and to consider whether any change in thinking has occurred during this session.

Distribute the article by Margaret Mead and Rhoda Metraux and the one by James Spaulding, Handouts 4 and 5. Ask participants to read them before Session 11.

Encourage further exploration of the Scripture passages, using the Bible-study tools listed in the bibliography in Session 2.

OPTIONAL ACTIVITY FOR SESSION 11

Ask for volunteers to participate in a debate as part of Session 11. Ask one-half of the group to develop an argument in favor of executing the man described in Handout 3, Session 11, a Case Study; ask the other half of the group to develop an argument against the execution.

OPINIONNAIRE ON THE DEATH PENALTY

(Please circle the number or word which best reflects your opinion)

	Strongly agree	Agree	Dis- agree	Strongly Disagree
1. Without the possibility of using the death penalty, government would be giving free rein to the murderous impulses of some of its members.	1	2	3	4
2. The use of the death penalty on the part of government is necessary to preserve community and justice.	1	2	3	4
3. Exodus 21:24 talks of an ''eye for an eye.'' Therefore, the state should use the death penalty in the case of heinous crimes.	1	2	3	4
4. There are some persons who are beyond redemption.	1	2	3	4

5. In the case of each of the following, do you feel that the death penalty should be used?

a) A person who kills a police officer while committing armed robbery.	Always	Sometimes	Never
b) A prisoner who kills a guard while trying to escape.	Always	Sometimes	Never
c) A prisoner who kills another prisoner.	Always	Sometimes	Never
d) A husband or wife who kills his or her spouse.	Always	Sometimes	Never
e) A parent who kills his or her child.	Always	Sometimes	Never
f) A rapist.	Always	Sometimes	Never
g) A person who kills several people by placing a bomb in a public place.	Always	Sometimes	Never
h) Someone who slowly tortured and finally killed his/ her victim.	Always	Sometimes	Never
i) A child molester.	Always	Sometimes	Never
j) An arsonist.	Always	Sometimes	Never
k) A nursing home proprietor who prescribes large quantities of dangerous drugs in order to collect Medicare funds.	Always	Sometimes	Never
l) A manufacturer who knowingly releases unsafe autos.	Always	Sometimes	Never
m) A driver impaired by alcohol who causes highway accidents.	Always	Sometimes	Never

INTERPRETING THE OLD TESTAMENT

Rabbi Judea B. Miller
Temple B'rith Kodesh
Rochester, New York

It is remarkable how some people who may normally ignore other biblical laws still insist on applying the biblical law of retribution, ". . . life for life . . . as he hath done, so shall it be done to him: breach for breach, eye for eye, tooth for tooth." (See Exodus 21:24.) They forget that the good book also provided the death penalty for Sabbath violators and for certain adulterers. According to Deuteronomy a child who is "stubborn and rebellious" may be stoned. Though I may have been tempted many times to stone my children when they got out of hand, fortunately this is a punishment we no longer use.

It is questionable among biblical scholars how these punishments were carried out. The Rabbinical commentaries point out that no two eyes are exactly alike. After all, who would dare compare his sight with that of a Picasso or a Chagall? Likewise, no two lives are exactly alike. Therefore it was concluded that the law of retribution was carried out in the form of equivalent monetary compensation to the victim or to the victim's survivors. Apparently when Shakespeare wrote the *Merchant of Venice,* he was unaware of this. There were so many restrictions to carrying out the death penalty in ancient Israel and Judah that by the time of the destruction of the Second Temple by the Romans in the year 70, it is believed that, in effect, the death penalty was been made virtually impossible in Jewish Law.

In a moving passage from the *Mishnah Sanhedrin,* an ancient rabbinical text, there is this description of the way one questioned a witness in a capital punishment case:

"How shall one impress witnesses in a criminal case with the gravity of their position? One takes them aside and charges them 'Be certain that your testimony is no guess work, no hearsay, not derived at second-hand, nor by reliance on the observation even of a trustworthy person. Remember, you must face a severe cross examination. Know that a criminal case is by no means like a civil. In the latter, he who has caused an injustice by his testimony can make monetary restitution, but in the former, the blood of the accused and this unborn offspring stain the perjurer forever. Thus, in the case of Cain, Scripture says, "The voice of the bloods of your brother call to Me." Observe that the text reads in the plural, not blood, but bloods. For Abel's blood and that of his unborn seed were alike involved. It is for this reason that God created only one human in the beginning, a token to man that he who destroys one life, it is as though he had destroyed all mankind; whereas he who preserves one life, it is as though he had preserved all men.' . . ."

USING BIBLICAL MATERIALS

Paul L. Hammer
Professor of New Testament
Colgate/Rochester
Bexley Hall/Crozer

Any valid concern for biblical materials calls not for a superficial ''proof texting'' that can use verses out of context; it calls for the kind of serious study that employs the best tools of biblical scholarship to seek the most accurate understanding possible.

Yes, there are texts that seem to support a retributive form of justice, that can refer to political authority as ''the servant of God to execute his wrath on the wrong-doer'' (from Romans 13, a section used even to support acquiescence with the Nazi regime). In this very difficult passage Paul does struggle with the purpose of the state *in that historical context*. Yet it is not an absolute word for all contexts anymore than is

''Happy shall he be who takes your little ones and dashes them against the rock!'' (Psalm 137).

Further, Paul's concern for the state here (Romans 13:1-7) is bracketed by more comprehensive exhortations: ''Repay no one evil for evil, but take thought for what is noble in the sight of all. . . . Do not be overcome by evil, but overcome evil with good'' (from Romans 12:17-21; see all of that chapter) and ''Owe no one anything, except to love one another; for he who loves his neighbor has fulfilled the law'' (Romans 13:8).

Thus in dealing with any specific texts we need to see them in their larger contexts, and ultimately in the context of the creating, liberating, and whole-making God who seeks to overcome all evil with good for the sake of all persons.

Crime: A Life for a Life—June, 1978

from *Aspects of the Present* by Margaret Mead and Rhoda Metraux

As Americans we have declared ourselves to be champions of human rights in the world at large. But at home . . .

At home the Congress and the majority of our state legislatures have been hurrying to pass new laws to ensure that persons convicted of various violent crimes (but not the same ones in all states) may be—or must be—executed.

In my view, it is a sorry spectacle to see a great nation publicly proclaiming efforts to modify violence and to protect human rights in distant parts of the world and at the same time devoting an inordinate amount of time and energy at every level of government to ensure that those men and women convicted of capital offenses will be condemned to death and executed. Decisions to carry out such vengeful, punitive measures against our own people would reverberate around the world, making a cold mockery of our very real concern for human rights and our serious efforts to bring about peace and controlled disarmament among nations.

If we do in fact take seriously our chosen role as champions of human rights, then certainly we must also reinterpret drastically the very ancient law of "a life for a life" as it affects human beings in our own society today. I see this as a major challenge, especially for modern women.

But first we must understand where we are now.

In the late 1960s we lived through a kind of twilight period when, without any changes in our laws, men and women were condemned to death but the sentences were not carried out. Those who had been condemned were left to sit and wait—often for years.

In 1972 there was a brief period when it seemed that capital punishment had finally been abolished in the whole United States, as it has been in most of the modern countries of western Europe and in many other countries. For then, in the case of *Furman v. Georgia,* the Supreme Court of the United States ruled that existing laws whereby certain convicted criminals were condemned to death were haphazard and arbitrary in their application and constituted cruel and unusual punishment, which is prohibited by the Eighth Amendment to the Constitution. True, the Court was divided; even the five justices who supported the ruling were quite sharply divided in their reasoning. Nevertheless, *Furman v. Georgia* saved the lives of 631 persons in prisons across the country who were under sentence of death.

It seemed that we had passed a watershed.

But we were quickly disillusioned. The Supreme Court had not yet abolished capital punishment; the justices merely had ruled out the discriminatory manner in which the current laws were applied. As Justice William O. Douglas pointed out in his concurring opinion, the existing system allowed "the penalty to be discriminatorily and disproportionately applied to the poor, the Blacks and the members of unpopular groups."

In response, lawmakers in many states—often pushed by their constituents and by law-enforcement agencies—tried to meet the objections by means of new and contrasting laws. Some of these laws made the death penalty mandatory; no exceptions or mitigating circumstances were possible. Others made the death penalty discretionary, that is, they provided very specific guidelines for defining mitigating circumstances that should be taken into account. The reason was that experts differed radically in their opinions as to what the justices of the Supreme Court would find acceptable in revised laws.

In their haste, these lawmakers missed their chance to think in quite other terms.

Meanwhile, of course, cases were tried and a few women and many men were once more condemned. In July, 1976, the principles underlying the new laws were tested as the Supreme Court of the United States announced rulings in five of these cases, upholding three discretionary death-penalty statutes and ruling against two that imposed mandatory capital punishment. As a result, the death sentences of 389 persons in 19 states were later reduced to life imprisonment.

But the lawmaking and the convictions have continued. At the end of 1977, the number of condemned prisoners in the death rows of penitentiaries in the 33 states that then had capital-punishment laws amounted to 407—five women and 402 men—divided almost evenly between white Americans and Black or Hispanic Americans. Two were Native Americans—Indians—and concerning six, even this meager background information was lacking. Most were poor and ill educated, too unimportant to be permitted to enter into plea bargaining and too poor to hire the expensive legal talent that makes possible very different treatment in the courts for more affluent and protected individuals.

In early 1977 one man, Gary Gilmore, whose two attempts at suicide were given extravagant publicity, finally was executed in the midst of glaring national publicity in the mass media. Looking back at this one sordidly exploited event, can anyone picture how we would react if, without discussion, it were suddenly decided to execute *all* the death row prisoners who were without resources to prolong their lives?

What we are much more likely to do, I think, is to seesaw between the old, old demand for drastic retribution for crimes against human beings that very rightly rouse us to anger, fear and disgust and our rather special American belief that almost everyone (except the suspected criminal we catch on the run and kill forthwith) is entitled to a second chance. So we make harsh laws, convict some of the people who break them—and then hesitate. What next?

Every month the number of those convicted, sentenced and waiting grows. Violent criminals, they become the victims of our very ambiguous attitudes toward violence and our unwillingness to face the true issues.

The struggle for and against the abolition of capital punishment has been going on in our country and among enlightened peoples everywhere for well over a century. In the years before the Civil War the fight to end the death penalty was led in America by men like Horace Greeley, who also was fighting strongly to abolish slavery, and by a tiny handful of active women like New England's Dorothea Dix, who was fighting for prison reform. In those years three states—Michigan in 1847, Rhode Island in 1852 and Wisconsin in 1853—renounced the use of capital punishment, the first jurisdictions in the modern world to do so.

Both sides claim a primary concern for human rights. Those who demand that we keep—and carry out—the death penalty speak for the victims of capital crimes, holding that it is only just that murderers, kidnapers, rapists, hijackers and other violent criminals should suffer for the harm they have done and so deter others from committing atrocious crimes.

In contrast, those who demand that we abolish capital punishment altogether are convinced that violence breeds violence—that the death penalty carried out by the State against its own citizens in effect legitimizes willful killing. Over time, their concern has been part of a much more inclusive struggle for human rights and human dignity. They were among those who fought against slavery and they have been among those who have fought for the civil rights of Black Americans, of immigrants and of ethnic minorities and Native Americans, for the rights of prisoners of war as well as for the prisoners in penitentiaries, for the rights of the poor, the unemployed and the unemployable, for women's rights and for the rights of the elderly and of children.

Now, I believe, we can—if we will—put this all together and realize that in our kind of civilization "a life for a life" need not mean destructive retribution, but instead the development of new forms of community in which, because all lives are valuable, what is emphasized is the prevention of crime and the protection of all those who are vulnerable.

The first step is to realize that in our society we have permitted the kinds of vulnerability that characterize the victims of violent crime and have ignored, where we could, the hostility and alienation that enter into the making of violent criminals. No rational person condones violent crime, and I have no patience with sentimental attitudes toward violent criminals. But it is time that we open our eyes to the conditions that foster violence and that ensure the existence of easily recognizable victims.

Americans respond generously—if not always wisely—to the occurrence of natural catastrophes. But except where we are brought face to face with an unhappy individual or a family in trouble, we are turned off by the humanly far more desperate social catastrophes of children who are trashed by the schools—and the local community—where

they should be learning for themselves what it means and how it feels to be a valued human being. We demean the men and women who are overwhelmed by their inability to meet their responsibilities to one another or even to go it alone, and we shut out awareness of the fate of the unskilled, the handicapped and the barely tolerated elderly. As our own lives have become so much more complex and our social ties extraordinarily fragile, we have lost any sense of community with others whose problems and difficulties and catastrophes are not our own.

We do know that human lives are being violated—and not only by criminals. But at least we can punish criminals. That is a stopgap way. But it is not the way out of our dilemma.

We also know that in any society, however organized, security rests on accepted participation—on what I have called here a sense of community in which everyone shares.

Up to the present, the responsibility for working out and maintaining the principles on which any code of law must depend and for the practical administration of justice has been primarily a male preoccupation. At best, women working within this framework have been able sometimes to modify and sometimes to mitigate the working of the system of law.

Now, however, if the way out is for us to place the occurrence of crime and the fate of the victim and of the criminal consciously within the context of our way of living and our view of human values, then I believe liberated women have a major part to play and a wholly new place to create for themselves in public life as professional women, as volunteers and as private citizens concerned with the quality of life in our nation. For it is women who have constantly had to visualize in personal, human terms the relationships between the intimate details of living and the setting in which living takes place. And it is this kind of experience that we shall need in creating new kinds of community.

Women working in new kinds of partnership with men should be able to bring fresh thinking into law and the administration of justice with a greater awareness of the needs of individuals at different stages of life and the potentialities of social institutions in meeting those needs. What we shall be working toward is a form of deterrence based not on fear of punishment—which we know is ineffective, even when the punishment is the threat of death—but on a shared way of living.

It will be a slow process at best to convince our fellow citizens that justice and a decline in violence can be attained only by the development of communities in which the elderly and children, families and single per-

sons, the gifted, the slow and the handicapped can have a meaningful place and live with dignity and in which rights and responsibilities are aspects of each other. And I believe that we can make a start only if we have a long view, but know very well that what we can do today and tomorrow and next year will not bring us to utopia. We cannot establish instant security; we can only build for it step by step.

We must also face the reality that as far as we can foresee there will always be a need for places of confinement—prisons of different kinds, to be frank—where individuals will have to be segregated for short periods, for longer periods or even, for some, for a whole lifetime. The fear that the violent person will be set free in our communities (as we all know happens all too often under our present system of law) is an important component in the drive to strengthen—certainly not to abolish—the death penalty. For their own protection as well as that of others, the few who cannot control their violent impulses and, for the time being, the larger number who have become hopelessly violent must be sequestered.

But we shall have to reconsider the whole question of what it means to be confined under some form of restraint, whether for a short period or for a lifetime. Clearly, prisons can no longer be set apart from the world. Prisoners must have some real and enduring relationship to a wider community if they are to have and exercise human rights. Whether as a way station or as a permanent way of living for a few persons, prison life must in some way be meaningful.

There is today a Prisoners Union, organized by former prisoners, as well as a variety of local unions within many prisons. We shall have to draw on the knowledge and experience of groups of this kind. Here again I believe that women, who have not been regularly and professionally involved in traditional prison practices, may be freer to think and construct new practices than male experts working alone.

The tasks are urgent and difficult. Realistically we know we cannot abolish crime. But we can abolish crude and vengeful treatment of crime. We can abolish—as a nation, not just state by state—capital punishment. We can accept the fact that prisoners, convicted criminals, are hostages to our own human failures to develop and support a decent way of living. And we can accept the fact that we are responsible to them, as to all living beings, for the protection of society, and especially responsible for those among us who need protection for the sake of society.

DEATH PENALTY BREEDS KILLERS

Rochester Patriot, June 22–July 12, 1977

by James Spaulding

(PNS)—With the recent upsurge in public sentiment favoring the death penalty, a growing number of critics are going on the counter-offensive with a claim that capital punishment may in fact be an invitation to murder.

William C. Bailey, a Cleveland State University sociologist, has surveyed crime statistics in 42 states and found that, on the average, more people kill each other in states that have the death penalty than in states without it.

This is true, he says, even allowing for regional, cultural and other differences.

For instance, in 1968 those states which had abolished the death penalty experienced an average of .21 first degree murders per 100,000 population.

States with capital punishment saw nearly three times as many first degree murders— 53 per 100,000.

Roughly the same statistical spread holds up for second degree murder, homocides and total murders.

STATE SUICIDE

The explanation, says Bailey and others, is that capital punishment offers certain types of deranged personalities an acceptable means of suicide.

The death penalty "becomes a promise, a contract, a covenant between society and certain . . . warped mentalities who are moved to kill as part of a self-destructive urge," says Dr. Louis Jolyon West, head of the department of psychiatry at the University of California at Los Angeles.

Experts disagree on why support for the death penalty so greatly increased in the past 10 years, but most say that a major reason is the increase in crimes of violence. A fearful public, they say, looks to the death penalty as the most effective deterrent.

Yet West claims that capital punishment "breeds more murder than it deters."

"These murders," he says, "are discovered by the psychiatric examiner to be—consciously or unconsciously—an attempt to commit suicide by committing homicide. It only works if the perpetrator believes he will be executed for his crime."

West says he knows of cases in which "the murderer left an abolitionist [non-death penalty] state deliberately to commit a meaningless murder in an executionist state, in the hope of forcing society to destroy him."

Gary Mark Gilmore, who was executed January 17 by a firing squad in Utah, is often cited as an obvious example.

Some of his prison psychiatrists said Gilmore sought out his own death by murdering two young men in senseless, execution-style slayings.

SEEKS DEATH

Following his conviction, Gilmore demanded the death penalty be carried out despite the many objections of his attorneys.

West cites other examples:

● In 1965, a Texas farmer walked into a roadside cafe with a shotgun and blasted to death an Oklahoma truck driver he has never seen before. He said later, "I was just tired of living."

● In 1964, a lifer in an Oklahoma prison escaped and went on a spree of violence. After he was recaptured he petitioned the court to have him electrocuted, complaining that the state had gone back on its word three years before when he pleaded guilty to a murder, but was spared.

● In 1958, James French killed a motorist who gave him a ride in Oklahoma. He asked for the death penalty, but his public defender successfully pleaded for a life sentence. Later, in state prison, he deliberately strangled his cellmate.

According to West, "During a psychiatric examination in 1965 French admitted to me that he had seriously attempted suicide several times in the past, but always 'chickened out' at the last minute."

Gilmore also attempted suicide while in prison, apparently afraid his execution would be further delayed.

"French's basic motive in murdering his inoffensive cellmate," West said, "was to force the state to deliver to him the electrocution to which he felt entitled and which he deeply desired."

In 1966, French became the only person to be executed in the U.S. that year.

LONG KNOWN

Many psychiatrists have long observed the intimate relationship between murder and suicide. West said that in England nearly half of all murders are followed by suicide attempts, of which two-thirds succeed.

Thus, about one-third of all murderers in England kill themselves.

In Denmark, some 40 percent of murderers kill themselves.

Dr. Bernard L. Diamond, a psychiatrist at the University of California, Berkeley, says the relationship has been known for at least 200 years.

He cites a Danish law dating from 1767 that provides there should be no capital punishment for "melancholy and other dismal persons" who murders "for the exclusive purpose of losing their lives."

Diamond said that a man he examined at San Quentin Prison in 1959 the day before his execution confessed, finally, that the reason he murdered three women was "for the express purpose of dying by legal execution."

The same convict told a state investigator that he had twice tried suicide before the murders, "but lacked the guts." He agreed to talk to Diamond the day before the execution only on the condition that the execution be carried out.

"It took three murders and an attempted fourth to complete his suicidal mission," Diamond later wrote in a psychiatry journal.

PRISON DETERRENT

"I asked him what he would have done," Diamond said, "if California had had no capital punishment. He answered, 'I would have had to go to another state where they did have capital punishment and do it all there.'"

Diamond says he is convinced that if the man had known he wouldn't be executed and would have been forced to serve time in prison (which he hated bitterly), he would have been unable to commit murder.

Diamond concedes that if capital punishment is eliminated, such people might still seek death in other ways, such as a shoot-out with police. For them, he says, suicide is difficult, if not impossible.

Despite the statistics, advocates of the death penalty remain convinced that it is an effective deterrent.

California State Senator H.L. Richardson, founder of Gun Owners of America and a leading advocate of the death penalty, says that "to deny the deterrence of the death penalty is to deny all cause and effect."

"Every man has a right to his own mental aberrations, and these psychologists and sociologists are no different than anybody else," says Richardson.

But Diamond and his colleagues counter that for every murder that might be prevented by capital punishment at least as many more will be incited.

SESSION 10—BACKGROUND READING

Thou Shalt Not Kill

Interpreting the Old Testament

Rabbi Judea B. Miller
Temple B'rith Kodesh
Rochester, New York

It is remarkable how some people who may normally ignore other biblical laws still insist on applying the biblical law of retribution, ". . . life for life . . . as he hath done, so shall it be done to him: breach for breach, eye for eye, tooth for tooth." (See Exodus 21:24.) They forget that the good book also provided the death penalty for Sabbath violators and for certain adulterers. According to Deuteronomy (21:18-21) a child who is "stubborn and rebellious" may be stoned. Though I may have been tempted many times to stone my children when they got out of hand, fortunately this is a punishment we no longer use.

It is questionable among biblical scholars how these punishments were carried out. The Rabbinical commentaries point out that no two eyes are exactly alike. After all, who would dare compare his sight with that of a Picasso or a Chagall? Likewise no two lives are exactly alike. Therefore it was concluded that the law of retribution was carried out in the form of equivalent monetary compensation to the victim or to the victim's survivors. Apparently when Shakespeare wrote the *Merchant of Venice,* he was unaware of this. There were so many restrictions to carrying out the death penalty in ancient Israel and Judah, that by the time of the destruction of the Second Temple by the Romans in the year 70, it is believed that, in effect, the death penalty had been made virtually impossible in Jewish law. A court that had sentenced even one person to die in seventy years was regarded as a "bloody court."

In a moving passage from the *Mishnah Sanhedrin,* an ancient rabbinical text, there is this description of the way one questioned a witness in a capital punishment case:

How shall one impress witnesses in a criminal case with the gravity of their position? One takes them aside and charges them, "Be certain that your testimony is no guess work, no hearsay, not derived at second-hand, nor by reliance on the observation even of a trustworthy person. Remember, you must face a severe cross examination. Know that a criminal case is by no means like a civil. In the latter, he who has caused an injustice by his testimony can make monetary restitution, but in the former, the blood of the accused and his unborn offspring stain the perjurer forever. Thus, in the case of Cain, Scripture says, 'The voice of the bloods of your brother call to Me.' Observe that the text reads in the plural, not blood, but bloods. For Abel's blood and that of his unborn seed were alike involved. It is for this reason that God created only one human in the beginning, a token to men that he who destroys one life, it is as though he had destroyed all mankind; whereas he who preserves one life, it is as though he had preserved all men."

Future generations may look back at the death penalty in our day with much the same revulsion that many of us now have when we consider how capital punishment was used in the Middle Ages. At that time the death penalty was carried out against many more criminals than now, including blasphemers, witches, and pickpockets. It was not uncommon in England, during the three centuries when to be a pickpocket was a capital offense, to have the pockets picked of the very crowds that had gathered to watch the executions. The death penalty then was no more a deterrent to pickpocketing than it is now to other crimes. Recognizing this, at least forty-five countries, including almost all the Western democracies, have abolished the death penalty. An exception among the Western democracies is the United States, where the death penalty still exists in many states and where it may soon be reintroduced into most of the other states.

The execution of Gary Gilmore by a firing squad in Utah in 1977 has reopened the debate about capital punishment. Gilmore insisted on his right to force the people of Utah to kill him; to make them murderers as he was. This was a temptation the state of Utah could not resist. There was a bizarre irony in the decision that came about the same time from a court in Texas to allow television networks to show actual executions. For if the death penalty is a deterrent to crime, then executions should be done in public. Indeed, they should be done on television during prime viewing time. School children should be taken to see them. For what good is a deterrent unless as many people as possible, especially the young, see it being carried out? There is no lesson in having it done without spectators. If this sounds barbaric, it is but a logical conclusion of the argument that the death penalty is supposedly a deterrent to murder.

But most of us know that the death penalty is in fact no deterrent. Gary Gilmore was executed, and still the muggings and murders and crimes of violence will not now decrease. On the contrary, there is abundant evidence to indicate that capital punishment is not a deterrent to crime—the taking of life by the state may well encourage a climate of violence. The death penalty cheapens our respect for human life and brutalizes the spirit of all of us.

There are some additional problems with capital punishment. The U.S. Supreme Court acknowledged in its decision in 1972, that threw out the then existing capital punishment laws, that the death penalty violated the principle of equal protection. For executions were carried out mainly against the poor, the black, the uneducated, and generally the pariahs of society. Former Supreme Court Justice William O. Douglas observed, ''One searches our chronicles in vain for the execution of any member of the affluent strata of this society.''

We forget that the law is just a human instrument. Human beings, even judges and juries, may make mistakes. The legal system is administered by a vast number of different people in different circumstances and may produce inequalities and errors. But the taking of a life is radically different from any other sort of punishment because it is final and irreversible. If there has been an error, the carrying out of an execution is beyond any correction. It is hoped that our states, therefore, will resist the temptation to revert to capital punishment and will seek better, more effective ways of dealing with crime.

But if it has been demonstrated that the death penalty does not really serve as a deterrent to crime, why should we even consider reintroducing it? One reason often heard is that capital punishment would at least show some sort of concern for the victim. But this is absurd because it will in no way undo the crime, nor does it benefit the victim. Nor is it demonstrated that it will prevent another person from committing a similar crime. All it does is add to the violence of the original crime, for executions cheapen life. If we are ever to still violence, we must learn to cherish life.

The gallows, the electric chair, the guillotine, the gas chamber, and the firing squad are not only instruments of death. Like the cross for crucifixion in the ancient Roman Empire, they are symbols of terror, cruelty, and irreverence for all life. The death penalty is a spiritual link between primitive savagery, medieval fanaticism, and modern totalitarianism. It stands for everything that humanity must reject if it is to be worthy of survival.

So why are our state legislatures now considering reintroducing the death penalty as punishment for certain crimes? I believe it is because more and more people are angry and frustrated by a siege mentality that has gripped our cities. It has been said that a ''conservative'' today is often just a ''liberal'' who has been mugged. In this desperate situation, people tend to lash out in a mindless, irrational way. The call for the reintroduction of the death penalty is such a result. But let us remember that the death penalty will not correct the situation.

On the contrary, a climate of violence may be encouraged by the taking of human life by the state. We understand the provocation and sympathize with the anger that prompts many to call for the death penalty. But the provocation and temptation to reintroduce capital punishment must be resisted. The crawl of humanity out of savagery has been long and difficult. We still have far to go. The angry call from the mob for blood revenge must be resisted; otherwise we revert to savagery.

SESSION 11—Greater Love Than This

SCRIPTURE: Luke 6:27, 28, 32-36;
Matthew 5:43-48

TIME: 45 minutes to 1 hour

OBJECTIVES

1. To have participants probe the moral concerns involved in the issue of the death penalty and to question its acceptability from the perspective of our Christian faith.

2. To provide participants with information about the ineffectiveness of the death penalty as a deterrent to crime and about its discriminatory application.

LEADER PREPARATION

Materials needed:

Bible

Advance Preparation

1. Prepare Newsprint Chart 1.

SESSION AT A GLANCE

Death Penalty Quiz	10 minutes
Discussion of Quiz and Assigned Readings	10 minutes
Jury Role Play	15 minutes
Discussion of Role Play	10 minutes
Scripture Reading	

---

2. Make copies of Handouts 1, 2, 3, and 4.

SESSION OUTLINE

Death Penalty Quiz (10 minutes)

Distribute copies of Handout 1, the Death Penalty Quiz. Allow 5 minutes for completion.

Distribute copies of Handout 2, the Answer Sheet. Allow up to 5 minutes for participants to check their answers.

Discussion of Quiz and Assigned Readings (10 minutes)

Encourage open discussion of the quiz and of the article by Margaret Mead and Rhoda Metraux and the one by James Spaulding, distributed in Session 10. Stimulate the discussion by questions such as these:

● Margaret Mead points out that nearly half of those on death row are members of minority groups and almost all of them are poor. How does this violate the *tsedeqah* notion of justice?

● James Spaulding contends that the death penalty breeds killers. What does he mean? How does the death penalty contribute to the tenor of violence in society?

● What information in the Answer Sheet was most surprising? Most disturbing?

Jury Role Play (15 minutes)

If your group is smaller than twelve, ask the entire group to serve as a ''jury.'' If it is larger, ask participants to break into groups of approximately twelve. Distribute copies of the Case Study, Handout 3. (If a group prepared in advance a debate on this case study, ask persons to present their arguments and follow up with the discussion as suggested below.) Explain that the person in the case study has been found guilty of first-degree murder. In compliance with a Supreme Court ruling requiring a separate jury to decide whether to impose the death penalty, each group is to role-play a jury deciding on whether to impose the death penalty, in light of the aggravating and mitigating circumstances of this case.

Each ''jury'' will be asked to report its decision at the end of 15 minutes.

Discussion of Role Play (10 minutes)

Ask for each decision. Reveal that the case study is that of Gary Mark Gilmore, executed by the state of Utah in 1977. Guide the discussion by these questions:

● What assumptions and what values undergirded your decision?

- Are such assumptions acceptable from the perspective of our Christian faith?
- How would a just (and caring) community respond?

Session Summary (2 minutes)

Ask someone to read aloud Matthew 5:38-46. Allow time for a brief silent meditation. Distribute copies of Handout 4, "Death Penalty Fact Sheet." If possible, distribute denominational statements on the death penalty.

DEATH PENALTY QUESTIONNAIRE

Directions: In the space provided before each statement, write *true* or *false*.

___ 1. Each year there are about 20,000 homicides. About 100 convicted murderers a year are sentenced to die because of their crimes.

___ 2. The murder rate in states that have abolished capital punishment is higher than that in comparable states which have retained the death penalty.

___ 3. Police officers on duty suffer a higher rate of criminal assault and homicide in states that have abolished capital punishment as compared to states that have retained it.

___ 4. It has been established that at least 70 innocent persons have been executed in the United States. Between 1889–1927, 12 percent of the 406 persons sent to Sing Sing for execution were sentenced in error. Because of the sophistication of our present jury system, it is unlikely that an innocent person would be condemned to death in this modern era.

___ 5. The race of the *victim* significantly affects the sentence the guilty person receives.

___ 6. Whether a person is sentenced to death has generally been independent of that person's income.

___ 7. Society would not be endangered if many first-degree murderers were paroled.

___ 8. Public executions would deter crimes of violence.

___ 9. There is a close relationship between murder and suicide.

___10. If the United States abolishes the death penalty, it will be the first country in the world to do so.

ANSWER SHEET FOR DEATH PENALTY QUESTIONNAIRE

1. *True*. ("The Case Against the Death Penalty," Bedau, 1977).
2. *False*. Studies have shown that in adjacent states, one having the death penalty and one not, the murder rate is similar. A comparison of the murder rate in Missouri, Colorado, and Kansas from 1920–1958 showed little difference. The rate of homicide in Kansas dropped in 1935 after the death penalty was reinstituted, but so did the rate in Missouri and Colorado, which had the death penalty right along. (Franklin E. Zimring and Gordon Hawkins, *Deterrence: The Legal Threat in Crime Control* [Chicago: University of Chicago Press, 1973], p. 265; Thorsten Sellin, "Homicides in Retentionists and Abolitionist States," in Thorsten, ed., *Capital Punishment*, 1967, p. 135.)
3. *False*. In Detroit between 1928–1948, police were assaulted and killed at a rate two-thirds that of Chicago. There were fifty-five executions carried out in Cook County during these years, none in Michigan. (See chapters by Thorsten Sellin and Donald Campion in Hugo A. Bedau, ed., *The Death Penalty in America* [New York: Doubleday & Co., Inc., 1964].)
4. *False*. Between 1974–1976 in North Carolina alone, fifteen persons sentenced to death were later found to be innocent. Four members of a motorcycle gang were convicted in 1975 in New Mexico and were awaiting execution when another man confessed to the murder. Fortunately, none of these persons was executed because of a delay caused by the Supreme Court's consideration of the constitutionality of the death penalty. (*Criminal Justice Issues*, vol. 3, no. 1, Sept., 1976.)
5. *True*. Blacks constitute 54 percent of murder victims. Only 13 percent of those on death row had black victims, 87 percent had white victims. (Riedel, in 49 *Temple Law Quarterly* 261, 1976.) A 1977 study in Florida, Georgia, and Texas showed that while 54 percent of murder victims there were black, only 5 percent sentenced to die had black victims.

6. *False*. Both Clinton Duffy, former warden at San Quentin, and Michael DiSalle, former governor of Ohio, agree that lack of money was a principal factor in people being condemned to death. A recent study showed that 60 percent of those on death row were unemployed at the time of their crime. Most were represented by appointed counsel; most of these lawyers had less than five years experience. (Riedel, in *Temple Law Quarterly*, 1976; *The Charlotte Observer*, April 1, 1974, p. 1.)
7. *True*. In New York, between 1930–1961, 63 first degree murderers were paroled. By the end of 1962, only one had committed another crime, a burglary. (John M. Stanton, "Murderers on Parole," in *Crime and Delinquency*, vol. 15, no. 1 (January, 1969), p. 150.)
8. *False*. At a public execution in 1949 in New Castle, Delaware, there was so much drunken brawling and outrageous violence that it led to all executions being commuted for the next nine years. Crowds became mobs and indulged in wild, unrestrained orgies after witnessing executions in both England and the United States. (Sol Rubin, *Law of Criminal Correction* [St. Paul: West Publishers, 1963], p. 323.)
9. *True*. Dr. Louis West, head of the Department of Psychiatry at UCLA states that the death penalty "becomes a promise, a contract, a covenant between society and certain warped mentalities who are moved to kill as part of a self-destructive urge." He cites various interviews with murderers in the U.S. About one-third of all murderers in England kill themselves, 40 percent in Denmark. (Spaulding, in the *Rochester Patriot*, June 22-July 12, 1977, p. 3.)
10. *False*. Canada abolished it in 1976; Great Britain abolished it except for treason in 1971. Only France and Spain have used it in the last decade in Western Europe. The United Nations' Economic and Social Council resolved that it is desirable to "progressively restrict the number of offenses for which the death penalty might be imposed, with a view to the desirability of abolishing this punishment."

CASE 7853612—A CASE STUDY

The Crime: During the robbery of a gas station, the attendant was ushered into the men's room and cold-bloodedly shot twice in the head.

The Victim: The attendant was a law student with a wife and baby.

The Murderer: At the time of the murder, the prisoner, age 36, was on a two-day drunken spree, precipitated by a rejection by his girl friend. The prisoner was the second of four sons born to a heavy-drinking, itinerant carpenter who was 47 at the time of the prisoner's birth. The prisoner's most vivid early memories were of long waits in bus stations as the family wandered through the West in search of work. As a child, the prisoner exhibited instability when he played "chicken" with trains on railroad trestles. He ran away at 12. At 14 he was sentenced to 18 months in reform school for stealing a car. His behavior after releases from reform school worsened. He had an explosive temper and was violence prone. Because of several robberies and a shooting he spent more time in prison.

Once he organized a suicide collective in prison. Several other inmates cut their wrists severely, but the prisoner only nicked his. Of one 15-year sentence, he served 9 years, most of that time in solitary confinement or in the prison hospital where he was sent after a serious suicide attempt. Testing showed the prisoner was of high average intelligence with ability in art and journalism. He was released from prison to attend art school, but on the day of release got drunk and held up a gas station. Altogether he had spent 18 of his 36 years behind bars.

When he was released the final time, the smallest adjustment baffled him. He found it difficult to buy clothes, make payments on a truck, or even go to the bathroom without asking permission. He turned to alcohol and painkillers, lost several jobs, and violated parole by leaving the area. He met a girl, lived with her, but was often abusive when drunk. Finally she left him, and in a drunken rampage he committed the crime in question.

Sample Legislative Guidelines Governing Sentences in Capital Crimes: After hearing all the evidence, the jury shall deliberate and render an advisory sentence to the court, based on the following matters:

● Whether sufficient aggravating circumstances exist;

● Whether sufficient mitigating circumstances exist which outweigh the aggravating circumstances found to exist.

The court, after weighing the aggravating and miti-gating circumstances, shall enter a sentence of life imprisonment or death. The sentence of death may only be imposed upon the concurrence of the jury and court.

Aggravating Circumstances

1. The capital felony was committed by a person under sentence of imprisonment.
2. The defendant was previously convicted of another capital felony or of a felony involving the use of threat of violence to the person.
3. The defendant knowingly created a great risk of death to many persons.
4. The capital felony was committed while the defendant was engaged or was an accomplice in the commission of or an attempt to commit or flight after committing or attempting to commit any robbery, rape, arson, burglary, kidnapping, aircraft piracy, or the unlawful throwing, placing, or discharging of a destructive device or bomb.
5. The capital felony was committed for the purpose of avoiding or preventing a lawful arrest or effecting an escape from custody.
6. The capital felony was committed for pecuniary gain.
7. The capital felony was committed to disrupt or hinder the lawful exercise of any governmental function or the enforcement of laws.
8. The capital felony was especially heinous, atrocious, or cruel.

Mitigating Circumstances

1. The defendant has no significant history of prior criminal activity.
2. The capital offense was committed while the defendant was under the influence of extreme mental or emotional disturbance.
3. The victim was a participant in the defendant's action or consented to the act.
4. The defendant was an accomplice in the capital felony committed by another person, and his participation was relatively minor.
5. The defendant acted under extreme duress or under the substantial domination of another person.
6. The capacity of the defendant to appreciate the criminality of his conduct or to conform his conduct to the requirements of the law was substantially impaired.
7. The age of the defendant at the time of the crime.

DEATH PENALTY FACT SHEET

"On January 17, 1977, Gary Mark Gilmore was killed by a firing squad in Utah and thereby became the first person to be legally executed anywhere in the nation in nearly ten years. That executions would resume was all but guaranteed when, six months earlier, the Supreme Court upheld the constitutionality of capital punishment. Thus, the national experiment with abolition of capital punishment is at least temporarily, at an end."[1]

Background

1972: The Supreme Court, in *Furman* v. *Georgia*, found that the use of discretionary death penalty laws violated the Eighth Amendment's prohibition against cruel and unusual punishment because it allowed the penalty of death to be applied in an arbitrary and capricious manner.

1976: In *Woodson* v. *North Carolina*, the court declared that mandatory sentences of death, which do not consider aggravating and mitigating circumstances, also violated the Eighth and Fourteenth Admendments.[2]

Simultaneously, in *Gregg* v. *Georgia*, the court declared that the death penalty was not *inherently* cruel and unusual.

DOES THE DEATH PENALTY DETER CRIME?

To date, no study has confirmed[3] that the death penalty has a deterrent effect on the rate of homicide. One study found that the use of the death penalty in a given state may actually increase the subsequent rate of homicide in that state.[4]

States which have restored the death penalty after abolishing it have not experienced a decrease in the murder rate after restoration. In Delaware, in fact, which restored the death penalty after abolishing it for three years, the rate increased following its restoration.[5]

Another study recently reported in the *Minnesota Law Review* found that there was no greater increase in the murder rate in those states which ceased using the death penalty in the 1960s than in those states that did not use it in the first place.

IS THE DEATH PENALTY APPLIED UNFAIRLY?

After the Furman decision, thirty-five states changed their laws so as to eliminate the arbitrary exercise of discretion of judge and jury and thereby reduce or eliminate the unequal proportion of indigent and nonwhite people being sentenced to death. However, a comparison of racial differences in people sentenced under pre- and post-Furman statutes revealed an actual increase in the proportion of nonwhites receiving the death penalty for murder from 53 percent nonwhite to 62 percent nonwhite.[6]

The race of the victim, as well as of the offender, is a significant factor. "Though blacks constitute 54% of murder victims, only 13% of the people on death row had black victims, while 87% had white victims."[7] A recent study indicated that *no* white has ever been executed when the victim was black.[8]

There is also strong evidence that the death penalty is applied disproportionately to the poor, unskilled, and uneducated. A study of persons on death row following Furman found that 62 percent were unskilled, service, or domestic workers, while only 3 percent were professional or technical workers; 60 percent were unemployed at the time of their crimes. Former Warden of San Quentin Prison, Clinton Duffey, who has witnessed over 150

---

[1]Hugo A. Bedau, *The Case Against the Death Penalty*, ACLU, 1977, p. 1.

[2]*New York Times*, November 15, 1977.

[3]Ehrlich, in an article which appeared in *American Economic Review* (1974), purports to show that for the years from 1933 through 1967, each additional execution in the United States might have saved eight lives. Subsequently, several qualified investigators have independently examined this claim, and all have rejected it. Cited in Bedau, *op. cit.*, p. 9.

[4]Bedau, *op. cit.*, p. 8.

[5]*Ibid*.

[6]*Ibid*.; also Thorsten Sellin, *The Death Penalty* (1959).

[7]Bedau, *op. cit.*, p. 13.

[8]*Southern Poverty Law Review*, November, 1977.

executions, declared that the death penalty is "a privilege of the poor."[9]

A MORAL ISSUE

Ultimately, persons of conscience must consider whether they wish their government to use death as an instrument of justice. We must ask ourselves if we wish to live in a society which considers all human life sacred, or one in which some lives are considered disposable. All must accept responsibility for the kinds of sanctions the state is allowed to impose for crime. Ultimately, then, the death penalty is a moral issue, the resolution of which will reflect the moral tenor of the people who live in this society.

[9]Bedau, *op. cit.*, p. 14.

WHAT YOU CAN DO

● Visit, call, or write to your state legislators urging them not to support any death penalty bill.

● Call or write your governor in support of his or her promise to veto any death penalty bill.

● Write a "letter to the editor" indicating your opposition to the death penalty.

● Urge your minister or rabbi to give a sermon on the sacredness of human life.

● Obtain statements and study materials from your denomination.

● Join the National Coalition Against the Death Penalty, 22 East 40th Street, New York, NY 10016

SESSION 11—BACKGROUND READING

Greater Love Than This

For all religious people, the moral question is at the center of the death penalty issue. Does the death penalty enhance the value of human life, or does it demean life? There are impassioned arguments on both sides of the question.

George Bernard Shaw wrote, "Murder and capital punishment are not opposites that cancel one another, but similars that breed their kind."[1]

"Philosophers and social scientists have long contended that the legal extermination of human beings in any society generates a profound tendency among the citizens to accept killing as a solution to human problems,"[2] says Louis West, head of the department of psychiatry at UCLA.

Justice Potter Stewart takes this view:

In part, capital punishment is an expression of society's moral outrage at particularly offensive conduct . . . . (Retribution is neither) a forbidden objective nor one inconsistent with our respect for the dignity of men. Indeed, the decision that capital punishment may be the appropriate sanction in extreme cases is an expression of the community's belief that certain crimes are themselves so grievous an affront to humanity that the only adequate response may be the penalty of death.[3]

One argument says that, when we take a life, we end the possibility of that person repenting, of becoming reconciled with God and neighbor.

Another says that, since murderers have not respected the lives of their victims, there should be no regard for their life.

Former Attorney General Ramsey Clark captures our dilemma:

Our emotions cry for vengeance in the wake of a horrible crime, but we know that killing the criminal cannot undo the crime, will not prevent similar crimes by others, doesn't benefit the victim, destroys human life and brutalizes society. If we are to still violence, we must cherish life.[4]

Charles L. Black, Jr., of the Yale Law School, paraphrased a passage in the Talmud, "Though the justice of God may indeed ordain that some should die, the justice of man is altogether and always insufficient for saying who these may be."[5] Yet, in too many countries, we humans take upon ourselves the burden of deciding who should live or die. We place more trust in the state, despite its frequent record of error, than we do in the ability of love to overcome evil.

Few people believe that *all* who kill should die in return. The material in Sessions 10 and 11 makes us keenly aware of the questionable aspects of the ways in which the decision to execute is reached.

No matter how many reasons may be proposed to justify capital punishment, execution remains society's revenge on those vulnerable enough to become tokens to a deterrence theory. Because the death penalty is so questionable on both legal and moral grounds, the United States should follow the lead of Canada and other countries which have abolished it. *A public informed about the discriminatory and sometimes erroneous application of the death penalty would not support state-sanctioned executions.*

Supreme Court Justice Thurgood Marshall explained his vote against capital punishment in 1972 by stating that "if the average citizen was fully aware of all of the

[1] George Bernard Shaw, quoted in Ramsey Clark, *Crime in America* (New York: Simon and Schuster, 1970), p. 332.

[2] Louis West, "Psychiatric Reflections on the Death Penalty," *American Journal of Orthopsychiatry,* vol. 45, no. 4 (July, 1975).

[3] Justice Potter Stewart, *Gregg* v. *Georgia,* 428 U.S. 153, 183-184 (1976).

[4] Ramsey Clark, quoted in Laurence J. Peter, *Peter's Quotations: Ideas for Our Time* (New York: Wm. Morrow Co., 1977), p. 142.

[5] Charles L. Black, Jr., quoted in Stephen Gettinger, *Sentenced to Die* (New York: Macmillan, Inc. 1979), p. 162.

varied facts involved in the capital punishment controversy, he would find it shocking to his conscience and to his sense of justice."[6]

Sessions 10 and 11 engage participants in factual and moral issues, as well as in biblical study. A brief examination of God's response to murderers in biblical accounts makes us keenly aware of God's pattern of redemption. In the first murder—that of Abel by Cain—God protected the murderer from those threatening him (Genesis 4:15; Deuteronomy 22:8; Isaiah 26:21). It was after Moses had killed an Egyptian and fled to Midian that he was called by God to lead the Israelites (Exodus 3). David, responsible for Uriah's death, became one of Israel's greatest kings and a sincere penitent (Second Samuel).

The only true sovereign is God. When the state makes life-and-death decisions, it is idolatrous because it places itself in the position of God.

When Christians advocate the death penalty, they are countering several key principles:

- that all human life is sacred;
- that the atonement was for all persons; and
- that no person is beyond redemption.

When the Old Testament legal code authorized the death penalty, it did so within very strict limitations on application. Further, that code must be put in its proper perspective in a biblical progression from advocacy of retaliation to advocacy of unlimited love and forgiveness. In the Wisdom Literature (Proverbs 24:10-12) the faithful are specifically told of their duty to save those about to be sentenced to death.

The Judeo-Christian ethic not only limits recourse to

---

[6] 408 U.S. at 369, cited in Stewart W. Karge, "Capital Punishment: Death for Murder Only," the *Journal of Criminal Law and Criminology*, vol. 69, no. 2 (Summer, 1978), p.184.

violence but also requires the abandonment of violent responses. If someone strikes you, not only do you not strike your assailant, but also you do not even ask for compensation.

Responding to evil with good is one significant way Christians can show their concern for God and neighbor. Imagine how empty the ethic of Jesus would be if he had struck his executioners dead.

Christians need never apologize for that ethic. To suffer others, even fools and maniacs, is more humane and godlike than to destroy them. The hope of redemption becomes for us the work of restoration.

To claim scriptural authority for capital punishment is to ignore the commands to give away coats as well as cloaks, to go two miles when prevailed upon to go one (Matthew 5:39-41).

It is hard to imagine how anyone could support the death penalty and sincerely pray, "Forgive us our trespasses." Jesus summed up the whole of the Law and the Prophets as doing to others what you would have them do unto you (Matthew 7:12; Luke 6:31).

For the Christian it is not enough to oppose killing. *The Old Testament concept of* tsedeqah *and Christ's teachings require active peacemaking:*

"If you love those who love you, what credit is that to you? For even sinners love those who love them. And if you do good to those who do good to you, what credit is that to you? For even sinners do the same . . . . But love your enemies, and do good, and lend, expecting nothing in return; and your reward will be great, and you will be sons of the Most High; for he is kind to the ungrateful and the selfish. Be merciful, even as your Father is merciful" (Luke 6:32-36).

SESSION 12—Alternatives to Prison

SCRIPTURE: Isaiah 61:1-3;
Luke 4:18-19

TIME: 45 minutes to 1 hour

OBJECTIVES

1. To expose participants to examples of alternatives to prison.

2. To encourage a stance of advocacy for alternatives to prison and to empower participants to adopt such a stance.

3. To encourage participants to stimulate their communities to put alternatives in place.

LEADER PREPARATION

Advance Preparation

1. Prepare Newsprint Chart 1.

SESSION AT A GLANCE

Advocating Alternatives
  Scenario and Task Assignment   (5 minutes)
  Meetings of Citizens' Committees
    and of Public Safety Committee (20 minutes)
  Legislative Hearing   (15 minutes)
Scripture Meditation   (5 minutes)

---

2. Make copies of Handouts 1, 2, 3, and 4.

3. It would be helpful to prepare a bulletin board of clippings about other models of alternatives and to encourage participants to contribute to it.

SESSION OUTLINE

Scenario and Task Assignment (5 minutes)

Divide the participants into four groups. This can be done by "counting off." Explain that in this session they will consider some possible alternatives to jail or prison. A basic assumption undergirding this session is that imprisonment is counterproductive to the view of justice as a standard for a caring community.

Read the following scenario:

(News Bulletin, Public Information Radio)—

Governor Rickey declared today, under his powers as state executive, a moratorium on the building of any new jails, prisons, or other forms of maximum security facilities.

The announcement comes at a time when this county finds itself hard pressed for a new jail. The present facility, located on South Wall Street, was built in 1895 and is beginning to show its age. The walls are so old that prisoners escaped last January by chiseling away the brick with forks and knives taken from the kitchen.

County Manager Arthur Bremmer said today, "The legislature has been in the process of studying the cost of a new jail; but now that we have the governor's declaration, I don't know what we'll do."

Gene Romera, of the Citizens' Group for the Development of Alternatives, has a different view of the situation. He said, "The legislature now has a responsibility to explore the numerous programs that, with adequate funding, could meet the county's needs and be far less costly than the construction of a new jail."

MEETINGS OF CITIZENS' COMMITTEES AND PUBLIC SAFETY COMMITTEE

Clarify the Tasks—For those in groups 1, 2, and 3 (Citizens' Committees):

● Your *tasks* will be to study the program and to develop a convincing argument in favor of your particular alternative.

● Your *goal* is to persuade the Public Safety Committee of the County Legislature (Group 4) to allocate funds for your alternative.

You will have only 20 minutes to develop your argument. Work quickly.

● Each group should select one person to serve as *spokesperson* for that group. That person will have 2 minutes to present the group's argument to the Public Safety Committee of the legislature and 3 minutes to answer questions from the Committee. *It is not necessary* for the spokesperson *to describe fully* the characteristics of his or her group's program, as it must be assumed that the legislature committee has already familiarized itself with each program.

● Each member of the group, in addition to the spokesperson, should be prepared to answer questions for the legislative committee or to help with clarifications. Thus, responsibility for this aspect of the task doesn't fall solely on the spokesperson but is shared by the entire citizens' committee. Try to anticipate the legislators' questions.

● Keep in mind that you will not be required to account for the entire jail population but only a portion of it, since we are assuming that a variety of alternatives will be considered by the legislature.

● Those of you who have been assigned to Group 4 will be playing the role of a member of the Public Safety Committee of the County Legislature.

● While the other groups are studying their respective programs, you will be studying all three programs and developing questions to be asked of the spokespersons following their presentations.

"Meetings" (20 minutes)

Distribute to each of the "Citizens' Groups" Handouts 1, 2, or 3, the description of the alternative they will be advocating. The "Public Safety Committee" should receive copies of all three programs.

Circulate among the groups, clarifying their tasks as needed. Since the Public Safety Committee has the most complicated task, you may want to work with them. Remind them that they have a special responsibility to maintain the safety of the community and that they should formulate their questions with this in mind.

Give a time signal after 15 minutes and remind each group that their spokespersons should soon be ready for the "Legislative Hearing."

"Legislative Hearing" (15 minutes)

Ask the "Public Safety Committee" to be seated at the front of the room, as in an actual hearing. "Convene" the Hearing by announcing the purpose for holding it and invite the spokesperson from Group 1 (Restitution) to present the argument for this alternative. Announce that there will be 2 minutes for the presentation and 3 minutes for questions from the members of the "Public Safety Committee." (You should adhere strictly to these time limits. A watch with a second hand would be helpful.)

After each of the spokespersons has presented his or her arguments, announce that the "Hearing" has adjourned.

Explain to the group that the alternative programs which they have been considering are not hypothetical but have been developed in various parts of the United States. The Restitution Program and the Halfway House were initiated in Minnesota. The Diversion from Court program is found in Rochester, New York. These are just a sampling of the kinds of alternatives that can help offenders remain in the community. With the prevailing prison system, virtually all prisoners return eventually to the community, often more bitter and alienated than before they were imprisoned. The community must then try to integrate them into its midst and restore them to its membership. These alternative approaches, then, may make the community's task more possible by avoiding the dangers of imprisonment. Unlike imprisonment, each of these alternatives requires the active involvement of offenders in the restoration of community and, hence, fosters a sense of responsibility.

Refer to the bulletin board, if you have collected articles about other alternatives.

Scripture Meditation (5 minutes)

Distribute copies of the Scripture Meditation, Handout 4, and allow participants to engage in individual reading and reflection.

the criminal justice process -- a chain of choices

POINT OF DISCRETION

1. LAW MAKING
2. INVESTIGATION
3. ARREST
4. ARRAIGNMENT
5. PRE-TRIAL CONSIDERATIONS-I
6. PRE-TRIAL CONSIDERATIONS-II
7. TRIAL SENTENCING
8. IMPLEMENTING OF SENTENCE
9. PAROLE HEARING

AGENT	LEGISLATOR	POLICE OFFICER	POLICE OFFICER	JUDGE	PROSECUTOR	DEFENSE ATT'Y, PROSECUTOR AND DEFENDANT	JUDGE AND/OR JURY	CORRECTIONAL OFFICIALS AND STAFF	PAROLE BOARD	RESULT
path to prison — EXERCISE OF DISCRETION	legislation to criminalize morality and minor discretions	decision to intervene	act to physically apprehend	setting of high-money bail	decision to let arrest charges stand	decision to plea bargain	If guilty, decision to incarcerate	disciplinary actions, probation revocation, loss of "good time"	decision to deny parole	WASTE, HIGH RECIDIVISM, A MYTH OF PUBLIC SAFETY, CLASS, RACE AND SEX DISCRIMINATION, 430,000 PERSONS INCARCERATED IN 5,500 INSTITUTIONS..."Crime School"
alternative path — EXERCISE OF DISCRETION	decriminalize	decision not to intervene	issue summons or citation	low-money bail, release on recognizance supervised release or diversion	lower charge from felony to misdemeanor, dismiss charges	speedy trial by judge and/or jury	If guilty—probation, fine, or suspended sentence; half-way community facilities; if innocent... freedom	no disciplinary actions, no revocation of parole	grant parole	MORE ECONOMICAL AND HUMANE TREATMENT OF OFFENDERS, LOWER RECIDIVISM, SAFER COMMUNITIES, FEWER PRISONERS IN FEWER PRISONS

discretionary justice

pick your spot for action -- but START with a MORATORIUM ON PRISON CONSTRUCTION

UUSC World Service

editor, Andrea M. Couture

The "UUSC World Service" is published three times a year by the Unitarian Universalist Service Committee as a supplement to "UU World". It is available on request to UUSC.

UNITARIAN UNIVERSALIST SERVICE COMMITTEE
78 Beacon Street, Boston, Mass. 02108

RESTITUTION CENTER

Purpose:
1. To repay victims of crime for their losses.
2. To confront the offender with the human impact of crime.
3. To change the victim's attitude toward the offender.
4. To release nondangerous offenders so they can support their families.
5. To deal with personal problems that may interfere with holding a job.

Selection: Male property offenders with no recent history of violence may apply to the center. They are screened by the staff and approved for release to the center by the department of corrections.

Program: The program has two elements:
1. Restitution
2. Dealing with problems so that the offender can hold a job.

A *contract* is signed upon entry to the program not only by the offender but also by the victim (if willing), parole board, and restitution staff member. It may include a requirement to participate in therapy for alcohol, drug, or other problems. A variety of therapeutic approaches is used:
1. Rewarding positive behavior
2. Individual and group counseling.

The program relies upon such *resources in the community* as mental health clinics and AA, rather than duplicating them in the facility. Men are encouraged to cement their ties to family and the outside world.

Facility: Twenty beds. Located on one floor of city YMCA.

Budget: $180,000 (plus earnings of men in program). Cost per resident per day is $14.50 as opposed to $16 in the state prison. Moreover, $5 a month is disbursed in restitution payments to victims or charities.

Funding: 60 percent from federal government (because this is a pilot). Remainder comes from state plus $13,000 a year from room and board charges to residents.

(N.B. Costs may not be realistic because of inflationary spirals. Adjust, if necessary.)

COMMUNITY RESIDENTIAL FACILITY

Purpose: Ultimate goal is to reduce criminal behavior. Immediate goal is to provide a less costly alternative to incarceration for adults and juveniles in need of residential program with some controls.

Selection: Any male over sixteen regardless of offense. Commitment requires *consent* of sentencing *judge*, offender, and a facility *screening committee* that includes one resident and one community member along with four professionals.

Program: Offenders may spend up to a year in this residential facility. They attend work or school, get intensive job and family counseling, help maintain and govern the facility, screen and treat new residents in group encounter sessions, set goals in a contract upon entry, and receive increasing independence according to tangible performance in such things as work, chores, or money management, contribute part of wages to room and board, and have *option of making restitution to the victim*. The program relies on resources in the community that otherwise would have to be duplicated within the facility, such as schools, vocational programs, mental health clinics.

Staff: An active volunteer program supplements the staff. In addition, fifteen live-in, unpaid counselors (mostly college students with an interest in careers in criminal justice or skills in counseling) serve as the custodial/corrections staff under the supervision of four professional staff.

Facility: Thirty beds. Would be housed in a former nurses' dorm on the grounds of the state hospital. Minimal capital investment necessary.

Budget: $116,000. Cost per resident per day is $13.50 as opposed to $16 in state prison and $35 in juvenile institution.

Funding: 73 percent from the state; 12 percent from residents; and 15 percent from county. Moreover, a new state law makes counties pay the full bill for its citizens committed to state prison. (This law is hypothetical.)

A DIVERSION FROM COURT PROGRAM

Purpose: To provide a program for a defendant *before* he or she even enters a plea may result in the dismissal of charges, making the regular court procedure unnecessary. If accepted, a defendant can participate in a program designed to give the opportunity to undertake job training, remedial education, job placement, or counseling. Successful completion of the program will likely result in charges being dropped and court prosecution avoided.

Selection: Referrals must be made by attorneys, either district attorney or defense lawyer. Eligibility is based on:

1. *Motivation*
2. *Need* for such a program
3. *Charge involved* (program limited to *first offenders* or those with prior minor record, where charge is misdemeanor or nonviolent felony.)
4. *Age 16* or over

Thus the program is quite selective and deals with those who have little previous contact with the law.

Program: Participants are screened by the staff; once accepted, are assigned to a counselor, who, after further interaction, refers client to an appropriate agency, i.e., Manpower for job training, or a mental health clinic.

A "performance contract" is drawn up, covering an initial period of about three months which may be extended. During this time, there is consistent supervision on part of the agency and the counselor as to the progress of the participant. If there is successful completion of the program, the charges may likely (though not necessarily) be dismissed upon recommendation from the pre-trial diversion staff. If not successful, there can be an extension of the time period, or a termination hearing, whereby a client could be dismissed from the program.

Staff Facility: Office space is needed. A director and three or four trained counselors, who have expertise in various areas of social services and are in contact with community resources/agencies so they can make the necessary referrals, could handle 40-60 intake clients per month.

Budget: $115,000. Per person much less than jail costs, but a little more than probation costs.

SCRIPTURE MEDITATION

The spirit of the Lord GOD *is upon me,*
  because the LORD *has anointed me;*
He has sent me to bring glad tidings to the lowly,
  to heal the brokenhearted,
To proclaim liberty to the captives
  and release to the prisoners,
To announce a year of favor from the LORD
  and a day of vindication by our God,
  to comfort all who mourn;
To place on those who mourn in Zion
  a diadem instead of ashes,
To give them oil of gladness in place of mourning,
  a glorious mantle instead of a listless spirit.
They will be called oaks of justice,
  planted by the LORD *to show his glory.*
            —Isaiah 61:1-3 (*The New American Bible*)

A portion of this passage is repeated by Jesus in the sermon which begins his ministry in Luke 4:18-19.

If we listen carefully to these words, what do they say to us about the fact that we imprison more people in the United States than do any other of the Western democratic nations?

We saw in Session 1 that God's justice is biased toward the poor and oppressed. It is to them that "glad tidings" are announced. Why is God's justice so biased?

In view of the fact that it is precisely the poor and oppressed who usually end up in prison, what should our response as Christians be toward the continued existence of prisons?

We have explored a concept of justice which requires that society's laws and institutions promote social harmony and facilitate the realization of each person's highest possible fulfillment. That is the definition of justice *(tsedeqah)* that is implicit in this passage.

How do the alternative programs which you considered in this session compare with imprisonment in terms of realizing justice?

SESSION 12—BACKGROUND READING

Alternatives to Prison

The State of Massachusetts pioneered the juvenile prison in 1846. One hundred and twenty-six years later, the state's Commissioner of Youth Services closed all such facilities. The juvenile prisons had been a failure; the time had come for a new approach.

Replacing prisons for Massachusetts' youth is a network of advocacy agencies, federally funded group homes, and secure units offering intensive treatment. Many youths receive help in solving their problems within their own neighborhoods from the Department of Youth Services.

Maine is currently experimenting with a similar program for its adult prisoners. Ninety percent of all females sentenced by the courts are assigned to a former juvenile institution where they receive remedial education up to the level of high school equivalency as well as vocational training.[1]

These examples of working alternatives to prison are important for several reasons. First, they indicate a widespread awareness in these states that prisons have not worked—a major premise of this book. Second, they show that agencies of the government and within the community are, in some places, not afraid to try creative solutions to the problem of crime. Third, they reject isolation and punishment in favor of keeping offenders as close as possible to their communities while helping them equip themselves to take direction of their own lives.

The point was made earlier that seldom does a prison experience develop in an offender a sense of responsibility for what he or she has done. Instead, those who have "served time" are likely to feel victimized themselves. In the same way, former prisoners tend to have lost ground in the vital area of directing their own lives. Virtually every aspect of prison life works against initiative and responsibility. In the best alternatives, the

[1] Report of the Fourth National Symposium on Law Enforcement, Science and Technology, Washington, D.C., May 3, 1972, p. 162.

offender is confronted with the reality of his or her own situation and is invited to improve it for the good of all.

What is needed to bring about widespread employment of alternatives? Surely it is not more money. Alternatives, with the possible exception of intensive psychiatric care, are considerably cheaper than the maintenance and expansion of the prison system. The cost benefit of alternatives can be as much as ten-to-one in nonresidential options and three-to-one in residential options.

The criminal justice system can be expected to respond positively to responsible advocacy for alternatives. Alternatives can answer the need of the community to be reasonably secure while, at the same time, respecting the personhood of the offender.

Is this coddling criminals? We think not. It makes sense to consult with offenders about their options because free and informed choices are always the best ones. Working out agreements rather than imposing punishment demonstrates the community's desire to see the offender succeed.

Respecting the humanity of the lawbreaker does not imply a naive refusal to restrict his or her freedom if it appears necessary. Some offenders will need the support and supervision available only in a community residential facility or halfway house.

The crucial element is a rebirth of neighborhood responsibility. Crime strikes at the heart of the community. The most effective response to crime lies within that same community. The high percentage of repeat offenses makes it clear that removing offenders from the community only sets the stage for a worse problem when they are released from prison. When citizens, as individuals and as groups, face up to the obligation to be concerned actively with *all* community members, a giant step will have been taken.

The church, as a responsible social institution, is found in every community. Session 12 asks church members to become advocates for community-based alternatives. In some communities this may be a new role for the church.

The church, in its relationship to offenders, has traditionally accepted the role of *visitor* but has often relegated it to an institutional chaplain. It is now time for the church to ask what *deeper connotation Christ gave to the word "VISIT."* Can the church react with indignation to dehumanizing situations born of years of citizen apathy and neglect?

Should the church be more faithful in assuming a *servant* role? Can it help to meet the needs of individual lawbreakers and their families? Can it be more aggressive in helping to meet the needs of victims and their families? Can it assist overburdened personnel to develop a more humane justice system?

When Jesus began his ministry by quoting from the prophet Isaiah (Isaiah 61:1-3; Luke 4:18-19), did he mean that the church should also assume the role of *liberator* of captives?

The spirit of the Lord has been given to me,
  for he has anointed me.
He has sent me to bring the good news to the poor,
  to proclaim liberty to captives
  and to the blind new sight,
  to set the downtrodden free,
  to proclaim the Lord's year of favor.
                              (The Jerusalem Bible)

The role of *liberator* for the church in this arena in modern times is only in the beginning stages of definition. Surely it will involve:

- liberation of the offender from defeating patterns of his or her own antisocial behavior,

- reduction of societal conditions which cause crime,
- liberation of our attitudes about lawbreakers so that we may move from a punitive orientation to a problem-solving approach, and
- establishment of alternatives in *our* communities.

Shortly after the tragic prison riots of the early 1970s, Jessica Mitford wrote in *Kind and Usual Punishment:*

When people come upon the celebrated statement of Eugene V. Debs—"While there is a soul in prison, I am not free"—they are prone to regard it as an affirmation of extraordinary human compassion. This it is.

But it also may be viewed as a profound social insight. And not only because the prison system, inherently unjust and inhumane, is the ultimate expression of injustice and inhumanity in the society at large. Those of us on the outside do not like to think of wardens and guards as our surrogates. Yet they are, and they are intimately locked in a deadly embrace with their human captives behind the prison walls. By extension so are we.

A terrible double meaning is thus imparted to the original question of human ethics: Am I my brother's keeper?[2]

As a response to the ethical dilemma Jessica Mitford poses, the church might ask not only, "Am I my brother's keeper?" but also "AM I MY BROTHER'S BROTHER?" and "AM I MY SISTER'S SISTER?" What does that mean?

If church members are convinced that we, as "keepers," have been unnecessarily harsh and arbitrary, we will want to find ways to be caring, healing, reconciling, and life giving.[3]

[2] Jessica Mitford, *Kind and Usual Punishment* (New York: Alfred A. Knopf, Inc., 1973), p. 297.
[3] Material on the role of the church adapted from *Am I My Brother's Keeper?* Judicial Process Commission, Rochester, New York, 1973.

SESSION 13—Restoration

SCRIPTURE: Leviticus 19:9-18

TIME: 45 minutes to 1 hour

OBJECTIVES

1. To raise the question of the respective responsibilities of offenders, victims, and community.
2. To help participants become aware that safer, caring communities require responsible participation.

LEADER PREPARATION

Materials needed:

Newsprint, markers

Advance Preparation

1. Prepare Newsprint Chart 1.

```
┌─────────────────────────────────────────────┐
│           SESSION AT A GLANCE                │
│ Community Accountability Panel    20 minutes │
│ Reflection and Small Group                   │
│     Discussion                    15 minutes │
│ Reporting and Total Group                    │
│     Discussion                    10 minutes │
└─────────────────────────────────────────────┘
```

2. Make copies of Handouts 1, 2, and 3.
3. Prepare Newsprint Chart 2.

SESSION OUTLINE

Community Accountability Panel (20 minutes)

Have the participants form "Community Accountability Panels" of from three to five persons. Distribute to each "panel" copies of the scenario and instructions, Handout 1.

Reflection and Small Group Discussion (15 minutes)

Distribute copies of the "Reflection and Discussion" sheet, Handout 2. Ask each "panel" to discuss the questions and to appoint a recorder who will share its decision about the action to be taken in the case it mediated and share the key points of its decision.

Reporting and Total Group Discussion (10 minutes)

Record the key points on Newsprint Chart 2.

```
┌─────────────────────────────────────────────┐
│              RESTORATION                     │
│                                              │
│ SANCTION DECIDED UPON:                       │
│ GOAL OF THE SANCTION:                        │
│                                              │
│ SIGNIFICANCE OF "ACCOUNTABILITY              │
│ PANEL":                                      │
│                                              │
│ IS YOUR RECOMMENDATION CONSISTENT            │
│ WITH "THE SPIRIT OF THE LAW"?                │
└─────────────────────────────────────────────┘
```

Distribute Handout 3.

COMMUNITY ACCOUNTABILITY PANEL

SCENARIO: You and the other members of your group are residents of an American city. Citizens in your community have sought and have achieved participation in many decision and policy-making aspects of local government. You have recently extended this participation to the criminal justice system. A person accused of a crime is now referred to the Community Accountability Panel in his or her neighborhood. These panels consist of persons who have knowledge of the conditions within their own neighborhoods, and of services available throughout the city. Your group is such a panel.

CASE: Joan, age 16, is accused of breaking into a home in your neighborhood. Nothing was taken, as the burglars ran out of the house when they heard someone approach.

The owner of the home explained to the panel that he and his wife had gone out for a ride, and when they returned, they found a window broken and their belongings ransacked.

Earlier in the day, a teenager who sometimes baby-sat for their children stopped by with two friends (Joan and Sue) and used their telephone because she was locked out of her own house. The home owner's hypothesis was that "the girls decided it was a nice house with some nice stuff. Together, they planned to come back and burglarize it."

When Joan was asked about the events described, she wept and said that it was the baby-sitter's idea. She claimed that she waited in the car outside the house. The baby-sitter no longer lives in the community.

TASK: You and the other members of the Accountability Panel must decide upon an appropriate sanction for Joan. A *sanction* is defined here as *an action* which is designed to establish the boundaries of acceptable behavior; affirms the just claims which have been violated; and establishes the responsibilities of the offending person, the victim, and the society for restoration of the community.

You will have 20 minutes to come to a group decision. One member of your panel should record the key points of your decision. This person will serve, also, as spokesperson for your group.

REFLECTION AND DISCUSSION

RESTORATION

"In short, what Americans should do about crime . . . must be especially to strengthen and defend the community continuously, and after a crime to restore its wholeness, with special concern for person most affected. That is what is meant by *social defense and restoration.*

"Not only does the individual offender need to change relationships with other people. The family, neighborhood, and larger community also need change. . . . The crime was a symptom of a fracture in community relationships. The criminal act has further disrupted the fabric of community. Criminal justice must address the brokenness of this social network and not only that of the individual offender's character and of his own social relations." (L. Harold DeWolf, *What Americans Should Do About Crime* [New York: Harper & Row, Publishers, Inc., 1976], p. 104.)

THE SPIRIT OF THE LAW

"When you reap the harvest of your land, you shall not reap your field to its very border, neither shall you gather the gleanings after your harvest. And you shall not strip your vineyard bare, neither shall you gather the fallen grapes of your vineyard; you shall leave them for the poor and the sojourner: I am the Lord your God.

"You shall not steal, nor deal falsely, nor lie to one another. And you shall not swear by my name falsely, and so profane the name of your God: I am the Lord.

"You shall not oppress your neighbor or rob him.

The wages of a hired servant shall not remain with you all night until the morning. You shall not curse the deaf or put a stumbling block before the blind, but you shall fear your God: I am the Lord.

"You shall do no injustice in judgment; you shall not be partial to the poor or defer to the great, but in righteousness shall you judge your neighbor. You shall not go up and down as a slanderer among your people, but you shall not stand forth against the life of your neighbor: I am the Lord.

"You shall not hate your brother in your heart, but you shall reason with your neighbor, lest you bear sin because of him. You shall not take vengeance or bear any grudge against the sons of your own people, but you shall love your neighbor as yourself: I am the Lord" *(Leviticus 19:9-18).*

QUESTIONS FOR DISCUSSION

1. What was the response (sanction) your panel decided upon and what was its goal?

2. What is the significance of the term "accountability panel"?

In what ways does this approach make the offender and the community accountable?

How does this compare to what happens when a judge imposes a sentence, particularly a sentence of imprisonment?

3. Are you convinced that your panel's recommendation is consistent with Dr. DeWolf's statement on social defense and restoration and with the Leviticus passage on "the spirit of the law"?

NEIGHBORS AS PEACEMAKERS: GOOD VERDICT

Citizen Panels Mediate
Crime, Nuisance Complaints

BY HARRIET STIX

SAN FRANCISCO—When Betty Parshall drove into her father's driveway one evening shortly before Christmas, she didn't pay much attention to the station wagon parked in front of John Thompson's house next door. She assumed, when half a dozen teen-agers ran from the house, piled into the station wagon and sped away, that they were relatives paying a visit.

But, in fact, Mrs. Parshall had come upon the scene of an attempted burglary. Looking back, she wonders if it was her arrival that broke it up. In any event, her mother had seen the youngsters, heard the sound of breaking glass and called the police.

Now, weeks later, Betty Parshall sits behind a table in the harshly lit Visitacion Valley Community Center. As a panel member of the neighborhood's Community Board, she will hear two cases on this Tuesday evening—one complaint of harassment, the other the break-in at Thompson's house.

That witness Parshall, who lives two doors from the Thompsons, should double as "judge" might seem questionable at the least. But the panel members are not really judges; they are mediators, intent on problem solving rather than the assignment of blame.

So it doesn't matter if the victim—or the perpetrator—is a friend or neighbor. In fact, the mediation program is based on the theory that community people can solve the problems of minor crimes and disputes better than the courts because they are neighbors.

"What is so good about this," Betty Parshall comments, "is that we are not establishing guilt or innocence. That makes us control our biases."

The mediation program is unique in that it is community rather than agency-based. Program director Raymond Shonholtz believes that has a number of advantages. In other models, he says, the mediator (and there is usually only one) has no relationship to the area or the people involved, and the mediator often has the power to impose a decision if the disputants cannot resolve it. "There is too much coercion," Shonholtz believes.

He says: "In our process, the community selects the panels, the panelists are all trained together and there are four or five on a panel. It's an open forum and the agreement is made with the panel as well as the disputants. Panelists can go out later and talk with the parties if they don't carry out what they said they would do."

Moreover, he suggests, in agency-tied programs there is no feedback, and people in the community miss a learning experience. Nor is there any outreach, so cases are heard only after the fact.

"But the prevention possible in a neighborhood program is extremely valuable," he says. "The problems can be reached at an early level when solutions are cheap."

From *Los Angeles Times, View,* Part IV, March 30, 1978.

SESSION 13—BACKGROUND READING

Restoration

We hear, from time to time, that one or more of the great museum treasures of our Western culture has been damaged by a flood or a theft. In all but the very worst of these situations there is hope, through skill and modern technology, of restoring the masterpiece to at least a semblance of its former brilliance. If efforts succeed, the work can be said to have been restored to all of us who share the culture of which it represents a highpoint. Often the costly, exacting work of restoration is carried out by an international team of experts pooling their talent. Funds are always forthcoming and one seldom hears complaints about the price being more than the painting or sculpture is worth.

Christians affirm that the "most lowly" person on earth is worth infinitely more to the Creator (see Luke 15:1-10) than all the best products of human talent and intellect. Might we not then, as religious persons, turn away from unjust and failing ways of dealing with erring brothers and sisters and instead pool our talents toward restoring the erring ones to the community? As a model we have the painstaking and creative efforts of those who restore Renaissance and other treasures. The keys to restoration are dedicated skill, an unwillingness to say the task cannot be done and a driving sense that, should they fail, something that is precious to the community will be lost.

Our work of restoration must be approached positively. For too long we have accepted the punitive response to law breaking. *In this curriculum we have discussed at length the failure of this punitive response and the need to try new solutions.* It is easy to become discouraged and say, "It's too difficult; it can't possibly be done." We must try. The stakes are too high for us to be defeated by real or apparent obstacles.

One overwhelming difficulty is the problem of sheer numbers. On any given day there are approximately 500,000 persons in jails and prisons in the United States. How can communities—however caring—deal with so many persons?

A first step is to examine the laws prohibiting so-called "victimless crimes" (see Session 3) and removing from the statutes offenses that are better handled in other ways. Decriminalization of "victimless crime" would diminish significantly the burden of local courts and jails. It would not only save tax money but would free personnel and energy for the larger task of handling more serious offenses. Most importantly, thousands of persons would be spared a senseless and potentially damaging encounter with the criminal justice system.

The dispute resolution model has the potential for handling the greatest number of cases in which there are aggrieved or injured parties. When groups of concerned, capable, and trained citizens come to grips with a crime, how will they deal with it? Uppermost in their minds will be, not how we punish the offender but how we can bring all parties together and heal this rupture to our whole community.

Unlike courts, which now concern themselves primarily with proof of guilt, citizen groups can look at *why* a dispute occurred. If chronic unemployment, lack of education, mental health problems, or similar factors enter in, they may be acknowledged and dealt with. This is perhaps the greatest advantage of this model over the adversarial, win-or-lose process of criminal court.

To judge is to discern. In Old Testament Hebrew a judge is a discerner (*dayyan*), a sifter (*palil*), or a magistrate (*shaphat*). In New Testament Greek to judge is to apply criteria (*krinō*). To discern, to sift, to apply criteria are to measure according to the scriptural, standard—the purpose of God. In scripture, all judges are those who represent God (*elohim*) and the function of judgment is considered necessary. When Moses spoke to the tribes of Israel, he said:

"And I charged your judges at that time, 'Hear the cases between your brethren, and judge righteously between a man and his brother or the alien that is with him. You shall not be partial in judgment; you shall hear the small and the great alike; you shall not be afraid of the face of man, for the judgment is God's; and the case that is too hard for you, you shall bring to me, and I

will hear it''' *(Deuteronomy 1:16-18).*

If "the judgment is God's," the goal is peacemaking, making right. Peace cannot be "made" without the involvement of the community. Neighbors cannot remain indifferent—the peaceful quality of their neighborhood is involved:

"You shall not hate your brother in your heart, but you shall reason with your neighbor, lest you bear sin because of him. You shall not take vengeance or bear any grudge against the sons of your own people, but you shall love your neighbor as yourself: I am the Lord" *(Leviticus 19:17-18).*

When strife occurs, the *elohim* (representatives of God) are called to action. Where human vulnerability is greatest, the church needs to be present.

It is clear that pursuing the goal of social restoration involves bringing together many talents, great determination, a sense of realism balanced by the faith that can move mountains. When we succeed, we shall have gone beyond the achievement of those superbly competent specialists who repair museum treasures of vast worth. We, in the joint effort of the community, offender and victim, shall have repaired a rent in the very fabric that holds our society together. And, far better than putting a painting or sculpture back on exhibit, we shall have contributed to a person's return to an active life in the community.

SESSION 14—The Need for a Vision

SCRIPTURE: Isaiah 65:21-25; Revelation 21:1-4

TIME: 45 minutes to 1 hour

PURPOSE: To experience the excitement of deciding the kind of future we would like to build.

OBJECTIVES

1. To enable participants to envision a society based on justice and on caring communities.

2. To empower participants to see such a vision as realizable.

LEADER PREPARATION

Materials needed:

Newsprint and markers
Paper and pencils
Bibles, or copies of Scripture quotations
Newsprint Chart from Session 6, "Elements of a Caring Community"

Advance Preparation

1. Make Newsprint Chart 1, Session at a Glance.

```
              SESSION AT A GLANCE
Imagining Exercise                         5 minutes
Building a Group Vision                    15 minutes
Comparison with Visions in Scripture       10 minutes
Reporting                                   5 minutes
Force-Field Analysis                        5 minutes
We Can Do It!                               5 minutes
```

2. Prepare Newsprint Charts 2 and 3.

SESSION OUTLINE

Imagining Exercise (5 minutes)

Ask each person to sit back, close his or her eyes, and relax. Tell participants to imagine the best society that they possibly can. Ask a series of questions, pausing between each one:

. . . What kind of government does your society have?
. . . What kind of economic structure does your society have?
. . . How are people educated in your society?
. . . What is the relationship between youth and older persons?
. . . Can you see the buildings, the neighborhoods?
. . . Can you imagine yourself, your family, and your friends in this society?

Tell them to let their imaginations run freely and to add to their "vision" any elements you have not mentioned.

Building a Group Vision (15 minutes)

Ask participants to gather into groups of three or four persons and to appoint a recorder. Have them compare and pool their personal visions, creating a group vision which combines the best elements of each personal vision.

Comparison with Visions in Scripture (10 minutes)

Distribute Bibles or copies of Isaiah 65:21-25 and Revelation 21:1-4 to each person. Ask persons in each group to discuss how their vision is like and how their vision is unlike these biblical visions. Again ask that the recorders be prepared to report the key points of this discussion.

Reporting (5 minutes)

Ask each recorder to share his or her group's vision with the total group and to tell, briefly, the key points of their discussion about how it compares with the biblical visions. You could call attention here to the Newsprint Chart from Session 6, "Elements of a Caring Community."

Force-Field Analysis (5 minutes)

Alvin Toffler, in *Learning for Tomorrow: The Role*

of the Future in Education, points out that the attitudes which we adopt toward the future are going to affect its shape. He says that there are three perspectives from which to view the future:

1. Given present trends and conditions, and minimal intentional intervention by persons, we can predict the probable future.

2. Given the present rate of technological and social change, and the various possibilities of human intervention, we can predict *possible* futures; and

3. If we have a vision, we can foresee and help to shape our *preferred* future.[1]

As Christians, we must consider what our *preferred* future is in the light of Christian values, and then we must work for its attainment. It is sometimes helpful to engage in force-field analysis, the purpose of which is to help us quickly to assess our strengths and weaknesses. It can empower us to work toward a goal when we discover that we have more strengths than we realized and that obstacles to changing conditions are not as insurmountable as they may have seemed.

Newsprint Chart 2

BUILDING THE FUTURE	
Obstacles – **Individual and Group**	**Strengths** + **Individual and Group**

Ask the participants to examine the list of negative forces. Combine them where possible. Try to determine which one discouraging force most needs to be addressed if your visions are to be achieved.

Have someone read the list of positive forces. Ask participants to give a shout of joy and to applaud the strengths!

Ask for comments on how the strengths of the group might be used to move in the direction of the visions.

[1] Alvin Toffler, ed., *Learning for Tomorrow: The Role of the Future in Education* (New York: Random House, 1974), Introduction and chapter 1.

We Can Do It!
Course Summary and Chant (5 minutes)

For about 3 minutes, ask participants to share what the course has meant to them.

Close with a chant used by Threshold volunteers who go into jails and prisons across the United States to counsel prisoners in decision-making skills. A guiding concept of Threshold is the idea that people can help shape their own futures.

The chant is repeated eight times. Each time a subsequent word is emphasized. Explain this to the group, and have them repeat the words once after you. Then ask everyone to stand and join in the group chant:

Newsprint Chart 3

> *WE* are the people who create the future!
> We *ARE* the people who create the future!
> We are *THE* people who create the future!
> We are the *PEOPLE* who create the future!
> We are the people *WHO* create the future!
> We are the people who *CREATE* the future!
> We are the people who create *THE* future!
> We are the people who create the *FUTURE*!

OPTIONS FOR EXTENDED SESSIONS

1. *Building a Group Vision*

Provide craft materials: clay, poster board, crayons, or paints, etc.

Ask each group to select from among the craft materials and, using these materials, to create an "art work" which portrays the group's vision. Ask them to take no more than 10 mintues to discuss and pool their personal visions, which will allow them about 20 minutes to prepare their visual presentation.

Post the "vision" of each group and let the total group react.

Do not discuss the Bible readings but use them as the basis for a minute of silent meditation.

Proceed with the force-field analysis.

2. For "Building a Vision," substitute "Instant Social Involvement" (By Waving the Magic Wand) from Design #3: Education for Social Responsibility, *Designs for Leader Development and Support,* a Doing the Word Resource of Joint Educational Development, pp. 22 and 23 (Church Education Services, 1101 InterChurch Center, 475 Riverside Drive, New York, NY 10115).

SESSION 14—BACKGROUND READING

The Need for a Vision

. . . we are short on the vision side and long on the reality side in our "can do," pragmatic, industrial society. We North Americans are doers and we hold little honor for visionaries and dreamers, which leaves all the apostles, saints and martyrs on the sidelines. This imbalance needs correction in our education for social change, because without a vision and clear alternatives we don't know what we stand for, and we don't know where the change we seek is going to end.[1]

Rooted as we all are in the everyday, it can be very difficult to move beyond the present to envision the future. If adults believe that dreaming is only for children, they deny their creative ability. If we become cynical about the possibility of the future being markedly better than the past or present, we succumb to apathy or despair. We need faith and hope to give us zest for the exercise of envisioning.

When biblical prophets most despaired that their people had lost their spiritual dimension and their moral integrity, they called them to a vision. *Isaiah's vision is captured most startlingly in the image of the wolf and the lamb grazing together; of the lion eating straw like the ox.* Isaiah and the author of Revelation envisioned a new age in which there are neither tears nor slavery; no more martyrdom or oppression; an age in which people will live in their own homes and eat the fruit of their own vineyards; when God will live with them as their consoler and champion.

Jeremiah was another Old Testament prophet who challenged the people of Israel to have faith in the future. And Jeremiah demonstrated through a symbolic act—his own faith—by purchasing a piece of property (a field) at Anathoth even though the land was under siege by the Babylonians (chapter 32).

Modern men and women have had visions of a better future set out for them in compelling ways. Martin Luther King, Jr., moved millions with his dream. Some of those millions took strength from that dream and dedicated themselves to the long struggle to bring about equality and harmony among the races. John F. Kennedy ignited a generation of young persons with his impassioned plea for a new age of mutual striving to eradicate social and economic evils at home and abroad. Thousands affirmed their belief in his dream by committing themselves to

[1]Charles R. McCollough, *Morality of Power* (Philadelphia: United Church Press, 1977), p. 78.

the Peace Corps or by active participation in the political process.

Although strides were made under such leaders, many of us find cynicism creeping in because of current problems which seem even more complex, even more resistant to solution than those of the fifties and sixties. Certainly the problems of criminal justice are among the most complex. Justice is not being done; neither are our citizens being protected.

Still, the passion for justice remains. Jeremiah's dilemma was the same as ours:

> If I say, "I will not mention him (God),
>   or speak any more in his name,"
> there is in my heart as it were a burning fire
>   shut up in my bones,
> and I am weary with holding it in,
>   and I cannot.
>
> —*Jeremiah 20:9*

If we are to be the people of God, we must respond to our yearning. ". . . let him hear what the Spirit says to the churches," wrote the author of Revelation (3:22). It appears that all citizens of the caring-community-to-be must make the difference. We in the church have a special responsibility to initiate change within our congregations. That change may begin as a new awareness of the problem of justice. It may blossom as individuals or a group make a concerted effort to effect change.

This book has suggested many small steps which could empower people to design helping institutions. To start at the grassroots, what about representative neighborhood councils to settle disputes and facilitate solutions for the familial and social problems that often lead to crime? These councils might cooperate with peace officers whose task would be to help prevent disputes by getting to the cause of the trouble.

As the vision grows, our preferred future would be one in which courts would exist only as forums of last resort. Places of restraint would exist only to prevent further violence. Staffing these homes would be persons whose function was to heal and to restore those restrained to their family and neighborhood.

If we dream of the "new age," encompassing the justice system would be a society dedicated to building each person. Any community, any governmental or educational agency would reflect this simple, positive but monumental commitment.

In our "new Jerusalem" children would be nurtured; each person would have dignity; the earth would not be ravaged; we would live together in trust.

Each generation must dream its own dreams, judge carefully to see if they be of God, and make a commitment toward realizing them—step by step.

"Justice as wholeness" is a compelling vision, meaning that justice has not been done if peace and security do not result. There can be no whole, no community, no covenant unless each part of the whole, each person, is included—in love.

> *In the wilderness justice will come to live*
> *and integrity in the fertile land;*
> *integrity will bring peace,*
> *justice give lasting security.*
>
> *My people will live in a peaceful home,*
> *in safe houses,*
> *in quiet dwellings.*
> *—Isaiah 32:16-18 (The Jerusalem Bible)*

Notes on Scripture

The Book of Revelation was written at a time when Christians were being persecuted by the Roman government for their beliefs. Most biblical scholars agree that it was composed during the reign of the Emperor Domitian (A.D. 81–96), who insisted that he be worshiped as a god. The author sought to strengthen the faith of the Christians by unraveling to them the meaning of their oppression and of their suffering. The lines of battle are drawn between Rome and the church—which the author portrays as led by Satan and Christ respectively—so there can be no doubt as to who will be the victor. The message of this book is one of both hope and resistance.

The "vision" which the author holds out to his brothers and sisters is beautifully described in 21:1-4. He encourages them not to despair; their faith can strengthen them to resist the principalities and powers of their society.

The Christian message is by its very nature one which compels us to envision a brighter—and a more just—future. Such is our hope and our promise, our comfort and our responsibility.

For further study, see:

D'Aragon, Jean Louis, S.J., in *The Jerome Biblical Commentary,* ed. Raymond E. Brown et al. Englewood Cliffs, N.J.: Prentice-Hall, Inc., 1969.

Gilmour, S. MacLean, in *The Interpreter's One-Volume Commentary.* Nashville: Abingdon Press, 1971, pp. 945-977.

Spivey, Robert A., and D. Moody Smith, Jr., *Anatomy of the New Testament.* New York: Macmillan, Inc., 1974, pp. 470-485.

See also John H. Westerhoff, *Tomorrow's Church: A Community of Change.* Waco, Texas: Word Books, 1976).

. . . we are short on the vision side and long on the reality side in our "can do," pragmatic, industrial society. We North Americans are doers and we hold little honor for visionaries and dreamers, which leaves all the apostles, saints and martyrs on the sidelines. This imbalance needs correction in our education for social change, because without a vision and clear alternatives we don't know what we stand for, and we don't know where the change we seek is going to end. (Charles R. McCollough, *Morality of Power* [New York: United Church Press, 1977], p. 64.)

"The passion for justice creates a longing for the time when persons 'shall beat their swords into plowshares, and their spears into pruning hooks.' Unless some visionary vitality is present, history gets bogged down in the status quo. The loss of vision turns society into the hands of cynics . . ." (Joseph C. Williamson, "Education for Justice," *Colloquy*, May-June, 1973, p. 18.)

". . . if we are convinced that we are innately evil, we will design the institutions of our culture according to that definition. Psychological definitions of the human state can thus become self-fulfilling prophecies. We may not be what we think we are, but what we think we are will determine in great part what we are to become. We must not design our future in terms of our current disillusionment, for those designs, even if erroneously conceived, will influence the future development of our species." (Willard Gaylin, "Caring Makes the Difference," *Psychology Today,* August, 1976, p. 39.)

We must work to build the kind of society in which it is easy for people to be good. (Peter Maurin, co-founder with Dorothy Day of the Catholic Worker Movement.)

RESOURCES (In addition to those cited in curriculum)

Available from: Criminal Justice Resource Center
New York State Council of Churches
3049 East Genesee Street
Syracuse, NY 13224

1) "Challenges to the Injustice of the Criminal Justice System" adopted by the National Council of Churches in November, 1979. Single copy 50¢ (This curriculum is designed to provide in-depth exploration of the issues raised in this policy statement.)

2) *Essays on Criminal Justice*—a publication of the National Interreligious Task Force on Criminal Justice. Single copy 40¢

3) *Community and Crime*—a statement of the Committee on Social Development and World Peace of the U.S. Catholic Conference. $1.00

4) *What Americans Should Do About Crime* by L. Harold DeWolf. Written from the perspective of Christian ethics, this book examines prevailing myths and misconceptions about crime; analyzes the historical, psychological, and sociological roots of crime; defines justice as social defense and restoration; and points to alternatives citizens can undertake in their own communities. New York: Harper & Row, Publishers, 1976. $3.95

What to Do About Crime by Frank W. Gunn. Leader's guide for discussion-action groups using DeWolf's book. New York: United Church Press, 1977. $1.95

5) *Educational Resources on Criminal Justice* A packet containing six basic workshops, three suggested liturgies, and a leader's guide. Stimulates education/action/reflection.

Leader's Guide	$1.00
"Crime and Its Victims"	.50
"Of Arrest and Arraignment"	.50
"Know Thy Rights" and "Scavenger Hunt"	.60
"Why Prisons" and "Why Not Alternatives"	.60
"Human Needs and Christian Response"	1.00

"Your Rights If Arrested"	.25
Judicial Process Commission, 1976	
Complete Set	$3.25

AUDIOVISUALS

6) "Alternatives for a Safer Society: New Responses to Crimes and Victims." A 25-minute slide cassette presentation produced by PREAP, New York State Council of Churches. Rental $7 + $5.00 postage and handling

7) "Changing View on Capital Punishment" (Filmstrip-Cassette). Is the death penalty "social justice" or "legalized murder"? Why have thirty-five states rewritten death penalty laws since 1972? Does it really deter crime? What are the moral implications of this issue? 80 frames, 15 minutes. Rental fee $3.00. New York Times Educational Enrichment Materials, 1978

8) "Once You Were Darkness, Now You Are Light" (Slide-Cassette). Depicts attitudes toward crime, the inequities of the criminal justice system, roles in which Christians can provide ministry. 17 minutes. Rental fee $3.00. Judicial Process Commission, 1973

9) "The American Penitentiary: An Experiment" (Slide Cassette). Presents the history of the penitentiary and the case for a moratorium on prison construction. 11 minutes, rental fee $3.00. National Moratorium on Prison Construction

For additional listings of books, pamphlets, and slide shows, request Resource List from New York State Council of Churches.

For other position papers and resources, contact your own denominational headquarters.

NEWSLETTER

Criminal Justice Update, 3 issues per year, National Interreligious Task Force on Criminal Justice, JSAC, 475 Riverside Drive, Room 1700A, New York, NY 10027.

CRIME AND COMMUNITY IN BIBLICAL PERSPECTIVE

"We cannot be in full community with God unless we also identify with and seek the good of all persons." This is a recurring theme throughout a fourteen-session study for adults and older youth which explores "justice as wholeness." Based on biblical study and scriptural references, this study addresses hard questions about criminal justice and grapples with the biblical implications of society's approach.

Group members analyze and evaluate criminal justice in light of Judeo-Christian perspectives concerning justice and the caring community. By developing a critical consciousness toward the Christian's relationships to God and his/her response to the world, each participant is led to envision a whole community in which the needs of persons are met and in which each person is empowered to find his/her highest possible fulfillment.

Crime and Community in Biblical Perspective is a thought-provoking curriculum for adult church school and an excellent study for weekly or Sunday night groups. This program resource book was developed by the Judicial Process Commission, an ecumenically sponsored agency in Rochester, New York. The Commission convened a group of Christian educators to serve as an editorial committee. This group wrote the foundation papers and served as a support group for the writers, Kathleen Madigan and William Sullivan.

Kathleen E. Madigan is Adjunct Associate Professor of Sociology at Monroe Community College. She previously served as an Adjunct faculty member at Nazareth College of Rochester, Empire State College, and Attica Prison (through Genesee Community College).

William J. Sullivan is Associate Professor, Department of Religious Studies, St. John Fisher College. He has contributed articles for several books, including *Beyond Survival* and *Liberation, Revolution, and Freedom.*

Cover design: Tom Williams

$9.50

0-8170-0904-3